DASH DIET COOKBOOK FOR BEGINNERS

1500 Days of Recipes to Get Healthy Once and For All with America's Favorite Diet to Lose Weight & Beat High Blood Pressure + 21 Days Meal Plan

BECCA RUSSELL

© Copyright 2022 - All rights reserved.

This document is aimed at providing accurate and reliable information regarding the subject at hand. The publication is sold because the publisher is not obligated to provide qualified, officially permitted or otherwise accountable services. If any advice is necessary, whether legal or professional, it should be ordered from a person with experience in the profession.

In no way is it legal to reproduce, duplicate, or transmit any part of this document in either electronic means or printed format. Recording of this publication is strictly prohibited and any storage of this document is not allowed unless with written permission from the publisher.

TABLE OF CONTENTS

TABLE OF CONTENTS

CHAPTER 4. APPETIZERS, SIDE DISHES AND SALADS

INTRODUCTION

By now it's common knowledge.

Cardiovascular diseases are the world's No.1 silent killer – for both men and women.

Unfortunately, these conditions mainly affect the heart, and their causes can differ.

But there is one in particular that is labeled by most studies as the "primary cause."

Why? Well... You just have to look at the numbers to see that.

In 2019, there were more than half a million deaths in the United States due to "this cause".

Just thinks that out of 68 million Americans, 1 in 3 adults suffer from it – and almost 20% are asymptomatic.

Unfortunately, "this cause" can also lead to other health problems, including heart attack, stroke, and heart failure.

So, what is it?

It's **hypertension** (aka high blood pressure).

You may have heard that:

- Only about 40% of hypertensive sufferers are successful in their efforts to keep it under control.
- Hypertension causes about 1,000 daily deaths.
- As mentioned before, about 20% of American adults with hypertension are not even aware that they have it.
- Almost 30% of American adults suffer from pre-hypertension, which is the early stage that precedes and signals the risk of hypertension.
- According to the latest figures, 69% of people who have their first heart attack, 77% of people who have their first stroke and 74% of people with chronic heart failure suffer from hypertension.

- In 2009, nearly 350,000 American deaths included hypertension as a primary cause or contributing factor.

And recent studies have shown that these numbers tend to increase if people don't improve their lifestyles.

Especially their diet.

In fact, obesity (or excessive weight) is among the main causes of hypertension, as confirmed by a study published in PubMed.

Therefore, overweight or obese people are at greater risk of having hypertension than normal weight individuals.

But thankfully, there is some good news.

Yep! Because in recent years – thanks to a single diet – thousands of Americans have solved their hypertension issues and lost pounds of fat in just a couple of weeks.

It's a diet that is capable of solving 2 problems at once, due to its simplicity and convenience.

So, if you also suffer from hypertension (or want to prevent it) and are looking for a definitive solution that also helps you lose weight without having to count calories or go hungry, then you are in the right place.

In fact, in this section, you will explore what has become known as the "DASH Diet."

You will learn all its advantages and why it has been ranked as the No.1 Diet in America.

Additionally, I will also share the 6 friendly foods to include in your diet, the foods you must avoid at all costs, and what the No.1 enemy of high blood pressure is.

So, are you ready for this?

Let's get started.

FIRST THING FIRST, SO LET'S START WITH THE NAME.

The term DASH stands for "Dietary Approaches to Stop Hypertension".

In fact, back in 1997, this diet was specifically developed as a nutritional approach to treating or preventing hypertension.

In addition, a recent study published in the American Journal of Preventive Medicine found that men and women under 75 who follow the DASH diet are less likely to have heart failure and hypertension than those on a standard American diet.

Incredibly, some 5.7 million adults in the United States have heart failure because of their hypertension – and about half of those who develop it die within five years of diagnosis.

I know, these figures can be scary, but don't worry, because thanks to this book you will learn the strategies that can protect your heart and reduce the hazards of hypertension.

But what is hypertension in the first place?

Arterial hypertension is a condition in which resting blood pressure is higher than a level considered normal.

So, your heart struggles to pump blood throughout your body, which further increases your blood pressure.

In fact, blood pressure is the "measure of the force that the heart deploys to pump blood through the body."

When measuring blood pressure, 2 values are taken into account:

- **Systolic pressure**: the pressure in the arteries when the heart beats.
- **Diastolic pressure**: the pressure in the arteries when the heart rests between beats.

Normal values are less than 120 systolic and 80 diastolic – also written as 120/80 mmHg. -

Experts consider you to have high blood pressure when these two values exceed 140/90 mmHg.

And as mentioned before, the higher your blood pressure levels, the higher the risk of other health issues such as heart disease, heart attack, and stroke.

And here's where the DASH Diet comes to the rescue.

But how does it work?

It's quite straightforward.

Just consider that *U.S. News* and *World Report* have ranked it as the "absolute best diet in America" and that it is endorsed by the National Heart, Lung, and Blood Institute.

Even research published in the Journal of American Medical Association confirms that the DASH diet is the best option to fight hypertension and weight loss.

Starting the DASH diet does not imply drastically changing your habits - quite the contrary. The changes that you need to make to your dining habits are minimal – and I'll tell you how about them in a moment.

Moreover, the DASH diet is known because it involves reducing the No.1 enemy of high blood pressure: salt (aka sodium).

We all know that consuming too much salt damages the heart, kidneys, and blood pressure - all major contributing factors to the most common cardiovascular diseases.

Why is excessive salt intake bad for you?

Because too much sodium in the bloodstream draws water into the blood vessels, which damages the artery walls.

And this increased pressure on the walls of the blood vessels leads to hypertension.

But don't panic, that doesn't mean you'll have to give up salt altogether – just reduce its consumption.

You see, according to the FDA, a standard American diet includes about 3,000/3,500 milligrams of salt a day.

By contrast, the DASH diet averages 1,500 to 2,300 milligrams per day.

But this varies depending on your situation.

In fact, based on your medical needs, you can choose from 2 different types of DASH Diet.

- The standard DASH diet: a dietary plan that limits sodium intake to 2,300 milligrams (mg) per day.
- The low-sodium DASH diet: a dietary plan that limits sodium intake to 1,500 mg per day (about 3-4 teaspoons).

To decide which one to adopt, you should consult your doctor.

YOU HAVE JUST SEEN WHAT THE DASH DIET IS AND WHY IT IS CONSIDERED THE BEST DIET IN AMERICA.

Yet maybe now you're wondering, "But how do I know if I have hypertension?"

As mentioned at the beginning, 20% of sufferers are asymptomatic and therefore show no warning signals of the issue. This is why blood pressure should be measured regularly.

However, when symptoms do occur, they may include:

- Morning headache.
- Nose bleeds.
- Irregular heart rhythm.
- Visual disturbances and ringing in the ears.

If you are in a state of severe hypertension, you may experience symptoms such as:

- Fatigue.
- Nausea.
- Vomiting.
- Confusion.
- Anxiety.
- Chest pain and muscle tremors.

If your blood pressure is not brought under control, there can be severe complications, such as:

- Chest pain (also called angina).
- Heart attack.
- Heart failure.
- Irregular heartbeat that can lead to sudden death.

That's why experts recommend following the DASH diet for the long term – and not just for weight loss.

Indeed, there are several other reasons to do so.

Are you wondering what I mean?

I mean that after 25 years of studies and research, scientists have discovered the hidden benefits offered by this diet.

What are they?

Let's take a look at them:

- It helps improve bone strength and prevent osteoporosis.
- It reduces the risk of developing cancer.
- It prevents cardiovascular diseases, as well as cerebrovascular diseases.
- It lowers the risk of gout by reducing uric acid levels in people with hyperuricemia.
- It decreases the likelihood of getting kidney stones.
- It helps prevent or control type 2 diabetes.
- It improves cholesterol levels.

Therefore, the DASH diet is a smart choice if you are looking for a balanced meal plan that includes a wide choice of nutritious and delicious foods – that you will soon find out what they are.

But first, let me tell you which ones you absolutely must avoid at all costs.

AS WE HAVE SEEN, RESEARCH SHOWS THAT REDUCING SALT IN THE DIET MEANS A LOWER RISK OF HYPERTENSION, HEART DISEASE, AND STROKE.

It is also true, however, that not adding salt to your food is one of the greatest challenges for those who follow the DASH diet.

Thankfully, though salt reduction is a core element of this diet, some alternatives allow you not to renounce the pleasure of your favorite foods.

But before we figure out how to accomplish that, let's see what foods are best avoided, and why...

Firstly, you should be aware that the instructions for following the DASH diet compiled by the National Institutes of Health point out that most of the sodium we consume comes through processed foods such as baked goods, some cereals, soy sauce, and even some antacids.

In fact, they suggest reading food labels to check the amount of sodium in different food products.

Therefore, you should be looking for foods that contain 5% or less of the daily allowance of sodium.

And as we've seen before, the daily sodium intake should be less than 2,300 milligrams (mg) per day.

Foods with 20% or more of the daily allowance of sodium are considered high-sodium foods.

So, what are the other main foods to avoid for your health?

Here they are:

1. Sweets and Added Sugar

Sweets include candy, sorbets, jellies, jams, sugary drinks, and cookies. Any sweets you do choose should be low-fat.

Those who consume little calories (especially the sedentary) should aim to avoid foods with added sugars. These may include sugary drinks, hard candy, jellies, and syrups.

Sedentary people should consume no more than five such sweets a week. On the other hand, those who play sports or lead an active lifestyle can consume up to two a day.

2. Fats and oil

In the DASH diet, you don't necessarily need to avoid fats and oils, but you should still limit their intake. For example, soft margarine, vegetable oil (such as corn, olive, or safflower), low-fat mayonnaise, or light salad dressings.

Try to limit the intake of these foods to two servings per day. Very active people, on the other hand, can consume up to three servings a day. A single serving is a teaspoon of oil or margarine, a tablespoon of mayonnaise, or two tablespoons of salad dressing.

Keep in mind, however, that the fat content of the food you choose affects the recommended serving size.

Let me explain better.

One tablespoon of normal salad dressing equals one serving. But one tablespoon of low-fat seasoning equals half a serving, and one tablespoon of fat-free seasoning equals zero servings.

3. Red meat (in excess)

Red meat is richer in saturated fat than the protein sources recommended in the DASH diet.

Therefore, red meat should be curtailed in this diet. There is no medically recommended amount as such, but experts recommend that if you usually eat large amounts of meat, you should try to reduce its consumption.

4. Alcohol

Adult drinks such as beer, wine, and spirits are not prohibited, but experts recommend curbing their intake. According to the guidelines, if you drink alcoholic beverages, do so in moderation.

Moderate consumption means no more than one drink per day for women and no more than 2 drinks per day for men.

5. Added salt

Remember what I said about salt?

That the primary goal of the DASH diet is to manage or reduce the risk of hypertension. Studies have shown that cutting down your salt intake can help reduce the risk of high blood pressure.

As a consequence, experts recommend not having the salt shaker on your table during meals and resisting adding salt to food.

Instead, use herbs, spices, lemon, lime, vinegar, wine, and unsalted seasoning blends in the kitchen to flavor the food.

And in addition to reducing the intake of these foods (or avoiding them) experts also recommend preventing hypertension or lowering blood pressure not only through food but also by adopting healthier habits.

Specifically, they recommend:

- Being physically active.
- Monitoring your healthy weight.
- Managing and coping with stress.

- Quitting smoking (including passive smoking).
- Sleeping at least 8 hours.

> **AS WE HAVE SEEN, YOUR GOAL WITH THE DASH DIET IS TO REDUCE YOUR SODIUM INTAKE TO 2,300 MILLIGRAMS PER DAY. ONCE YOU REACH THAT LEVEL, TALK TO YOUR DOCTOR TO FURTHER REDUCE IT TO 1,500 MILLIGRAMS PER DAY.**

And as mentioned before, most Americans consume about 3,400 milligrams of sodium a day.

And guess where all this salt comes from?

As mentioned before, it mostly comes from processed foods.

In fact, when grocery shopping for DASH diet foods, there is a trick to look for low-sodium foods.

The trick is to read the labels on the package and check the sodium content of the product. There are several "wordings" or "phrases" that you can find on the package.

They include:

- **Sodium-free or salt-free** means that the food contains less than five milligrams per serving.
- **Very low sodium** means that the food contains 35 milligrams or less of sodium per serving.
- **Low sodium** means that the food contains 140 milligrams or less of sodium per serving. Just consider that a low-sodium meal contains 140 milligrams or less of sodium per 3-1/2 ounce (100 gram) serving.
- **Light in sodium** means that the food contains 50% less sodium than its standard counterpart.
- **Unsalted or without added salt** means that no salt was added to the product during processing (this is not a sodium-free food).

So, the general advice is to check the label before buying any product.

That said, in addition to being low in sodium, the DASH diet is also rich in potassium and other minerals that help control blood pressure.

In fact, the "friendly foods" that I will reveal to you shortly are rich in potassium, magnesium, and calcium.

Why so?

For the following reasons:

- **Potassium** reduces the tension in the arteries and helps eliminate excess sodium from the body.
- **Magnesium** increases the production of nitric oxide, which contributes to opening up the arteries allowing easier blood flow.
- **Calcium** helps the blood vessels shrink and relax as needed.

In which foods are these minerals found?

Here they:

1. Grains

By grains I mean bread, cereals, pasta, and rice. When following the DASH diet, opt for whole grains (such as brown bread or brown rice) rather than refined cereals (such as white bread, white pasta, white rice, etc.).

Also, as mentioned before, read the labels carefully, because some breakfast cereals and baked goods are high in sodium.

However, you can consume six to eight servings of grains a day and active people can consume up to 11 servings per day. One serving means one slice of bread, 3/4 cup of dry cereal, or 1/2 cup of cooked cereal, rice, or pasta.

2. Vegetables

Try to eat vegetables such as broccoli, carrots, cabbage, green beans, peas, lima beans, and spinach – either cooked or raw.

You can buy fresh, frozen, or canned vegetables; but again, canned products may be high in sodium, so read the labels before you buy. Avoid frozen vegetable mixes that include high-fat, high-sodium sauces.

In addition, you should eat three to five servings of vegetables each day. Active people can have up to six servings. One serving of vegetables equals a cup of raw leafy vegetables or half a cup of chopped vegetables.

3. Fruit

In the DASH diet, fresh and dried fruit is recommended as well as fruit juice.

Apples, apricots, bananas, dates, grapes, oranges, grapefruit, or grapefruit juice all are excellent options.

You can buy fresh, frozen, or canned fruit.

Try to consume four to five servings of fruit each day. Active people can have up to six servings.

One serving of fruit is a medium whole fruit, half a cup of fresh, frozen, or canned fruit – but watch the label for sugar content of canned fruit, 1/4 cup of dried fruit, or 1/2 cup of fruit juice.

4. Dairy products

Choose fat-free dairy products. Avoid whole milk, butter, cream, and cheese.

Look for low-fat products like yogurt and milk. You'll need to reduce most of the cheese because usually, it isn't just high in fat, but it's also high in sodium.

However, try to consume two or three servings of skimmed milk or low-fat dairy products every day. Active people can have up to three servings. One serving means a cup of milk or yogurt.

5. Lean meat, poultry, and fish

Eat fish and seafood, or skinless chicken and turkey. Cut down on red meat and choose only lean cuts. All meats should be cooked without heavy sauces and should preferably be grilled or steamed.

Try to consume three to six servings of lean protein each day. Active people can have up to six servings. Sedentary people should consume less.

Keep in mind that eggs are high in cholesterol, so you should limit your egg yolk intake to no more than four per week. Besides, keep in mind that two egg whites have the same protein content as a slice of meat.

6. Nuts, seeds, and legumes

Nuts and seeds are good for you, but they're rich in fat, so be sure to keep an eye on portion sizes when consuming this king of foods. We recommend almonds, hazelnuts, sunflower seeds, and peanut butter. Keep in mind that seasoned nut mixes are often very rich in sodium and should therefore be avoided.

Legumes such as beans, lentils, and split peas are good protein sources while being low in fat. Yet canned beans usually contain more sodium than recommended.

Try to consume three to five servings a week. Active people, on the other hand, can consume one serving a day. One serving is ⅓ of a cup.

> **WE HAVE SEEN WHAT THE DASH DIET IS, HOW IT CAN PREVENT OR REGRESS HYPERTENSION, AND WHY IT HAS BEEN RANKED FOR YEARS AS "THE BEST DIET IN AMERICA."**

I also told you about the hidden benefits that this diet can offer, and how you can use them to your advantage.

Plus you have learned what foods to cut or avoid, and what foods to add to your shopping list instead.

Now, the time has come to check out the recipes I have compiled for you.

All you need to do is decide on the dishes you want to eat, and enjoy your new healthier lifestyle.

Chapter 1

BREAKFAST RECIPES

1
Pumpkin Cookies

🥣	🕐	👥
10 minutes	25 minutes	6

Ingredients

- 2 cups of whole wheat flour
- 1 cup of old-fashioned oats
- 1 teaspoon of baking soda
- 1 teaspoon of pumpkin pie spice
- 15 ounces of pumpkin puree
- 1 cup of coconut oil, melted
- 1 cup of coconut sugar
- 1 egg
- 1/2 cup of pepitas, roasted
- 1/2 cup of cherries, dried

Directions

1. Mix the flour the oats, baking soda, pumpkin spice, pumpkin puree, oil, sugar, egg, pepitas, and cherries in a bowl, stir well, shape medium cookies out of this mix, arrange them all on a baking sheet, then bake for 25 minutes at 350°F. Serve the cookies for breakfast.

Nutrition: Calories: 362; Carbohydrates: 46.7 g; Fats: 16.3 g; Protein: 7.2 g

2
Cinnamon and Pumpkin Porridge Medley

10 minutes

15 minutes

2

Ingredients

- 1 cup of unsweetened almond/coconut milk
- 1 cup of water
- 1 cup of uncooked quinoa
- 1/2 cup of pumpkin puree
- 1 teaspoon of ground cinnamon
- 2 tablespoons of ground flaxseed meal
- Juice of 1 lemon

Directions

1. Take a pot and place it over medium-high heat.
2. Whisk in water, and almond milk and bring the mix to a boil.
3. Stir in quinoa, cinnamon, and pumpkin.
4. Reduce heat to low and simmer for 10 minutes until the liquid has evaporated.
5. Remove from the heat and stir in flaxseed meal.
6. Transfer porridge to small bowls.
7. Sprinkle lemon juice and add pumpkin seeds on top.
8. Serve and enjoy!

Nutrition: Calories: 286; Fats: 6.3 g; Carbohydrates: 49.1 g; Protein: 8.2 g

3
Buckwheat Crepes

8 minutes

15 minutes

6

Ingredients

- 1 cup of buckwheat flour
- 1/3 cup of whole-grain flour
- 1 egg, beaten
- 1 cup of skim milk
- 1 teaspoon of olive oil
- 1/2 teaspoon of ground cinnamon

Directions

1. In the mixing bowl, mix up all ingredients and whisk until you get a smooth batter.
2. Heat up the non-stick skillet on high heat for 3 minutes.
3. With the help of the ladle pour the small amount of batter into the skillet and flatten it in the shape of a crepe.
4. Cook it for 1 minute and flip on another side. Cook it for 30 seconds more.
5. Repeat the same steps with the remaining batter.

Nutrition: Calories: 126; Carbohydrates: 21.4 g; Fats: 2.5 g; Protein: 4.5 g

4
Avocado Cup with Egg

5 minutes

0 minutes

4

Ingredients

- 4 teaspoon of low-sodium parmesan cheese
- 1 chopped stalk scallion
- 4 dashes of pepper
- 4 dashes of paprika
- 2 ripe avocados
- 4 medium eggs

Directions

1. Preheat the oven to 375°F. Slice avocados in half and discard the seed. Slice the rounded portions of the avocado to make it level and sit well on a baking sheet.
2. Place avocados on a baking sheet and crack one egg in each hole of the avocado. Season each egg evenly with pepper and paprika. Bake for 25 minutes or until eggs are cooked to your liking. Serve with a sprinkle of parmesan.

Nutrition: Calories: 221; Carbohydrates: 3.3 g; Fats: 19.4 g; Protein: 8.8 g

5
Spinach Muffins

10 minutes

30 minutes

6

Ingredients

- 6 eggs
- 1/2 cup of non-fat milk
- 1 cup of low-fat cheese, crumbled
- 4 ounces of spinach
- 1/2 cup of roasted red pepper, chopped
- 2 ounces of low-sodium prosciutto, chopped
- Cooking spray

Directions

1. Mix the eggs with milk, cheese, spinach, red pepper, and prosciutto in a bowl. Grease a muffin tray with cooking spray, divide the muffin mix, introduce it to the oven, and bake at 350°F for 30 minutes. Divide between plates and serve for breakfast.

Nutrition: Calories: 118; Carbohydrates: 3.9 g; Fats: 5.8 g; Protein: 13.2 g

6
Grapes & Kale Smoothie

 10 minutes   0 minutes   2

Ingredients

- 1 cup of seedless green grapes
- 2 cups of fresh kale, trimmed and chopped
- 1 tablespoon of fresh lime juice
- 3-4 drops of liquid stevia
- 1 1/2 cups of filtered water
- 1/4 cup of ice cubes

Directions

1. In a high-powered blender, place all listed ingredients and pulse until smooth and creamy.
2. Transfer the smoothie into two serving glasses and serve immediately.

Nutrition: Calories: 75; Carbohydrates: 16.1 g; Fats: 0.2 g; Protein: 1.3 g

7
Blackberry and Apple Smoothie

 5 minutes   20 minutes   2

Ingredients

- 2 cups of frozen blackberries
- 1/2 cup of apple cider
- 1 apple, cubed
- 2/3 cup of non-fat lemon yogurt

Directions

1. Add the listed ingredients to your blender and blend until smooth.
2. Serve chilled!

Nutrition: Calories: 153; Fats: 2.9 g; Carbohydrates: 25.1 g; Protein 7.3 g

8
Avocado & Spinach Smoothie

10 minutes   0 minutes   2

Ingredients

- 2 cups of fresh baby spinach
- 1/2 avocado, peeled, pitted and chopped
- 1 tablespoon of hemp seeds
- 1/2 teaspoon of ground cinnamon
- 3-4 drops of liquid stevia
- 2 cups of chilled filtered water

Directions

1. In a high-powered blender, place all listed ingredients and pulse until smooth and creamy.
2. Transfer the smoothie into two serving glasses and serve immediately.

Nutrition: Calories: 139; Carbohydrates: 6.1 g; Fats: 10.7 g; Protein: 5.1 g

9
Pineapple Smoothie

10 minutes   0 minutes   2

Ingredients

- 2 cups of pineapple, chopped
- 1/2 teaspoon of fresh ginger, peeled and chopped
- 1/2 teaspoon of ground turmeric
- 1 1/2 cups of cold green tea
- 1/2 cup of ice, crushed

Directions

1. In a high-powered blender, place all listed ingredients and pulse until smooth and creamy.
2. Transfer the smoothie into two serving glasses and serve immediately.

Nutrition: Calories: 133; Carbohydrates: 31.8 g; Fats: 0.3 g; Protein: 0.9 g

10
Raspberry Smoothie

10 minutes   0 minutes   2

Ingredients

- 1 cup of fresh raspberries
- 4 ounces of firm silken tofu, pressed and drained
- 4-5 drops of liquid stevia
- 1 1/2 cups of unsweetened almond milk
- 1/4 cup of ice, crushed

Directions

1. In a high-powered blender, place all listed ingredients and pulse until smooth and creamy.
2. Transfer the smoothie into two serving glasses and serve immediately.

Nutrition: Calories: 104; Carbohydrates: 10.2 g; Fats: 4.6 g; Protein: 5.4 g

11
Creamy Oats, Greens & Blueberry Smoothie

4 minutes   0 minutes   1

Ingredients

- 1 cup of cold fat-free milk
- 1 cup of salad greens
- 1/2 cup of fresh frozen blueberries
- 1/2 cup of frozen cooked oatmeal
- 1 tablespoon of sunflower seeds

Directions

1. Blend all ingredients using a powerful blender until smooth and creamy. Serve and enjoy.

Nutrition: Calories: 291; Fats: 6.2 g; Carbohydrates: 45.2 g; Protein: 14.8 g

12
Satisfying Berry and Almond Smoothie

10 minutes   **0 minutes**   **1**

Ingredients

- 1 cup of blueberries, frozen
- 1 whole banana
- 1/2 cup of almond milk
- 1 tablespoon of almond butter
- Water as needed

Directions

1. Add the listed ingredients to your blender and blend well until you have a smoothie-like texture.
2. Chill and serve.
3. Enjoy!

Nutrition: Calories: 85; Fats: 3.4 g; Carbohydrates: 11.2 g; Protein: 2.5 g

13
Salmon and Egg Scramble

15 minutes   **4 minutes**   **4**

Ingredients

- 1 teaspoon of olive oil
- 3 organic whole eggs
- 3 tablespoons of water
- 1 minced garlic
- 6 ounces of smoked salmon, sliced
- 2 avocados, sliced
- Black pepper to taste
- 1 green onion, chopped

Directions

1. Warm-up olive oil in a large skillet and sauté onion in it. Take a medium bowl and whisk eggs in it, add water and make a scramble with the help of a fork. Add to the skillet the smoked salmon along with garlic and black pepper.
2. Stir for about 4 minutes until all ingredients get fluffy. At this stage, add the egg mixture. Once the eggs get firm, serve on a plate with a garnish of avocados.

Nutrition: Calories: 235; Carbohydrates: 3.3 g; Fats: 19.1 g; Protein: 12.9 g

14
Chia Seeds Breakfast Mix

8 hours   **0 minutes**   **4**

Ingredients

- 2 cups of old-fashioned oats
- 4 tablespoons of chia seeds
- 4 tablespoons of coconut sugar
- 3 cups of coconut milk
- 1 teaspoon of lemon zest, grated
- 1 cup of blueberries

Directions

1. In a bowl, combine the oats with chia seeds, sugar, milk, lemon zest, and blueberries, stir, divide into cups and keep in the fridge for 8 hours.
2. Serve for breakfast.

Nutrition: Calories: 289; Carbohydrates: 53.8 g; Fats: 5.1 g; Protein: 7.3 g

15
Breakfast Fruits Bowls

10 minutes   **0 minutes**   **2**

Ingredients

- 1 cup of mango, chopped
- 1 banana, sliced
- 1 cup of pineapple, chopped
- 1 cup of almond milk

Directions

1. Mix the mango with the banana, pineapple, and almond milk in a bowl, stir, divide into smaller bowls, and serve.

Nutrition: Calories: 172; Carbohydrates: 34.1 g; Fats: 2.1 g; Protein: 3.7 g

16
Banana Bread

15 minutes | 60 minutes | 14

Ingredients

- Vegetable oil cooking spray
- 1/2 cup of brown rice flour
- 1/2 cup of amaranth flour
- 1/2 cup of tapioca flour
- 1/2 cup of millet flour
- 1/2 cup of quinoa flour
- 1/2 cup of raw sugar
- 3/4 cup of egg whites
- 1/8 teaspoon of iodized salt
- 1 teaspoon of baking soda
- 2 tablespoons of grapeseed oil
- 2 pieces of mashed banana

Directions

1. Preheat the oven to 350°F. Coat a loaf pan with a vegetable oil cooking spray, dust evenly with a bit of flour, and set it aside. In a bowl, mix the brown rice flour, amaranth flour, tapioca flour, millet flour, quinoa flour, and baking soda.
2. Coat a separate bowl with vegetable oil, then mix eggs, sugar, and mashed bananas. Pour the bowl of wet fixing into the bowl of dry fixing and mix thoroughly. Scoop the mixture into the loaf pan. Bake within an hour.
3. To check the doneness, insert a toothpick in the center of the loaf pan; if you remove the toothpick and it has no batter sticking to it, remove the bread from the oven. Slice and serve immediately and store the remaining banana bread in a refrigerator to prolong shelf life.

Nutrition: Calories: 102; Carbohydrates: 15.7; Fats: 2.7 g; Protein: 3.8 g

17
Pear & Greens Smoothie

| 10 minutes | 0 minutes | 2 |

Ingredients

- 2 large pears, peeled, cored, and chopped
- 2 cups of fresh mustard greens, trimmed and chopped
- 1/4 teaspoon of ground cinnamon
- 1 1/2 cups of filtered water
- 1/4 cup of ice cubes

Directions

1. In a high-powered blender, place all listed Ingredients and pulse until smooth and creamy.
2. Transfer the smoothie into two serving glasses and serve immediately.

Nutrition: Calories: 153; Carbohydrates: 34.8 g; Fats: 0.4 g; Protein: 2.3 g

18
Pumpkin Muffins

| 15 minutes | 20 minutes | 4 |

Ingredients

- 4 cups of almond flour
- 2 cups of pumpkin, cooked and pureed
- 2 large whole organic eggs
- 3 teaspoons of baking powder
- 2 teaspoons of ground cinnamon
- 1/2 cup of raw honey
- 4 teaspoons of almond butter

Directions

1. Preheat the oven to 400°F. Line the muffin paper on the muffin tray. Mix almond flour, pumpkin puree, eggs, baking powder, cinnamon, almond butter, and honey in a large bowl.
2. Put the prepared batter into a muffin tray and bake for 20 minutes. Once golden-brown, serve and enjoy.

Nutrition: Calories: 384; Carbohydrates: 27.2 g; Fats: 24.5 g; Protein: 13.2 g

19
Sweet Berries Pancake

15 minutes **15 minutes** **4**

Ingredients

- 4 cups of almond flour
- Pinch sea salt
- 2 organic eggs
- 4 teaspoons of walnut oil
- 1 cup of strawberries, mashed
- 1 cup of blueberries, mashed
- 1 teaspoon of baking powder
- Honey for topping, optional

Directions

1. Take a bowl and add almond flour, baking powder, and sea salt. Take another bowl and add eggs, walnut oil, strawberries, and blueberries mash. Combine the ingredients of both bowls.
2. Heat a bit of walnut oil in a cooking pan and pour the spoonful mixture to make pancakes. Once the bubble comes on the top, flip the pancake to cook from the other side. Once done, serve with the glaze of honey on top.

Nutrition: Calories: 386; Carbohydrates: 17.3 g; Fats: 28.6 g; Protein: 13.8 g

20
Quinoa Bowls

10 minutes **20 minutes** **2**

Ingredients

- 1 peach, sliced
- 1/3 cup of quinoa, rinsed
- 2/3 cup of low-fat milk
- 1/2 teaspoon of vanilla extract
- 2 teaspoons of brown sugar
- 12 raspberries
- 14 blueberries

Directions

1. Mix the quinoa with the milk, sugar, and vanilla in a small pan, simmer over medium heat, cover the pan, cook for 20 minutes and flip with a fork. Divide this mix into 2 bowls, top each with raspberries and blueberries and serve for breakfast.

Nutrition: Calories: 197; Carbohydrates: 39.1 g; Fats: 1.3 g; Protein: 7.6 g

21
Refreshing Mango and Pear Smoothie

 10 minutes   0 minutes   1

Ingredients

- 1 ripe mango, cored, and chopped
- 1/2 mango, peeled, pitted, and chopped
- 1 cup of kale, chopped
- 1/2 cup of plain Greek yogurt
- 2 ice cubes

Directions

1. Add pear, mango, yogurt, kale, and mango to a blender and puree.
2. Add ice and blend until you have a smooth texture.
3. Serve and enjoy!

Nutrition: Calories: 273; Fats: 3.2 g; Carbohydrates: 53.1 g; Protein: 7.9 g

22
Mixed Berries Smoothie

 10 minutes 0 minutes 2

Ingredients

- 1 cup of fresh strawberries, hulled and sliced
- 1/4 cup of fresh raspberries
- 1/4 cup of fresh blackberries
- 1 cup of fresh orange juice
- 1/2 cup of ice cubes

Directions

1. In a high-powered blender, place all listed ingredients and pulse until smooth and creamy.
2. Transfer the smoothie into two serving glasses and serve immediately.

Nutrition: Calories: 1.2; Carbohydrates: 22.1 g; Fats: 0.7 g; Protein: 1.8 g

23
Orange Smoothie

10 minutes **0 minutes** **4**

Ingredients

- 2/3 cup of rolled oats
- 2 large oranges, peeled, seeded and sectioned
- 2 large frozen bananas, peeled and sliced
- 2 1/2 cups of unsweetened almond milk
- 1 cup of ice cubes

Directions

1. In a high-powered blender, place all listed ingredients and pulse until smooth and creamy.
2. Transfer the smoothie into four serving glasses and serve immediately.

Nutrition: Calories: 189; Carbohydrates: 29.6 g; Fats: 5.3 g; Protein: 4.9 g

24
Apple & Kale Smoothie

10 minutes **0 minutes** **2**

Ingredients

- 1 green apple, peeled, cored, and chopped
- 1 frozen banana, peeled and sliced
- 1 Medjool date, pitted and chopped
- 2 cups of fresh baby kale
- 1 tablespoon of chia seeds
- 2 cups of chilled filtered water

Directions

1. In a high-powered blender, place all listed ingredients and pulse until smooth and creamy.
2. Transfer the smoothie into two serving glasses and serve immediately.

Nutrition: Calories: 149; Carbohydrates: 27.4 g; Fats: 2.6 g; Protein: 3.2 g

25
Kiwi & Cucumber Smoothie

10 minutes

0 minutes

2

Ingredients

- 2 kiwis, peeled and chopped
- 1 medium cucumber, peeled and chopped
- 2 tablespoons of fresh cilantro leaves
- 1/2 teaspoon of fresh ginger, peeled and chopped
- 2-3 drops of liquid stevia
- 2 cups of filtered water

Directions

1. In a high-powered blender, place all listed ingredients and pulse until smooth and creamy.
2. Transfer the smoothie into two serving glasses and serve immediately.

Nutrition: Calories: 59; Carbohydrates: 11.4 g; Fats: 0.6 g; Protein: 1.9 g

Chapter 2
LUNCH RECIPES

26
Rosemary Roasted Chicken

15 minutes	20 minutes	8

Ingredients

- 8 rosemary springs
- 1 minced garlic clove
- Black pepper
- 1 tablespoon of chopped rosemary
- 1 chicken
- 1 tablespoon of organic olive oil

Directions

1. In a bowl, mix garlic with rosemary, rub the chicken with black pepper, the oil and rosemary mix, place it inside a roasting pan, introduce it inside the oven at 350°F, and roast for sixty minutes and 20 min. Carve chicken, divide between plates and serve using a side dish. Enjoy!

Nutrition: Calories: 104; Fats: 4.5 g; Carbohydrates: 1.6 g; Protein: 14.3 g

27
Healthy Chicken Orzo

15 minutes   **15 minutes**   **4**

Ingredients

- 1 cup of whole wheat orzo
- 1 pound of chicken breasts, sliced
- 1/2 teaspoon of red pepper flakes
- 1/2 cup of feta cheese, crumbled
- 1/2 teaspoon of oregano
- 1 tablespoon of fresh parsley, chopped
- 1 tablespoon of fresh basil, chopped
- 1/4 cup of pine nuts
- 1 cup of spinach, chopped
- 1/4 cup of white wine
- 1/2 cup of olives, sliced
- 1 cup of grape tomatoes, cut in half
- 1/2 tablespoon of garlic, minced
- 2 tablespoons of olive oil
- 1/2 teaspoon of pepper
- 1/2 teaspoon of salt

Directions

1. Add water to a small saucepan and bring to a boil. Heat 1 tablespoon of olive oil in a pan over medium heat. Season chicken with pepper and salt and cook in the pan for 5-7 minutes on each side. Remove from pan and set it aside.
2. Add orzo into the boiling water and cook according to the packet directions. Heat remaining olive oil in a pan on medium heat, then put garlic in the pan and sauté for a minute. Stir in white wine and cherry tomatoes and cook on high for 3 minutes.
3. Add cooked orzo, spices, spinach, pine nuts, and olives and stir until well combined. Add chicken on top of orzo and sprinkle with feta cheese. Serve and enjoy.

Nutrition: Calories: 420; Fats: 21.7 g; Protein: 32.6 g; Carbohydrates: 23.2 g

28
Grilled Mahi-Mahi with Artichoke Caponata

 15 minutes 30 minutes 4

Ingredients

- 2 tablespoons of extra-virgin olive oil
- 2 celery stalks, diced
- 1 onion, diced
- 2 garlic cloves, minced
- 1/2 cup of cherry tomatoes, chopped
- 1/4 cup of white wine
- 2 tablespoons of white wine vinegar
- 1 can of artichoke hearts, drained and chopped
- 1/4 cup of green olives, pitted and chopped
- 1 tablespoon of capers, chopped
- 1/4 teaspoon of red pepper flakes
- 2 tablespoons of fresh basil, chopped
- 4 (5- to 6-ounce of each) skinless mahi-mahi fillets
- 1/2 teaspoon of kosher salt
- 1/4 teaspoon of freshly ground black pepper
- Olive oil cooking spray

Directions

1. Warm-up olive oil in a skillet over medium heat, then put the celery and onion and sauté for 4 to 5 minutes. Add the garlic and sauté for 30 seconds. Add the tomatoes and cook for 2 to 3 minutes. Add the wine and vinegar to deglaze the pan, increasing the heat to medium-high.
2. Add the artichokes, olives, capers, and red pepper flakes and simmer, reducing the liquid by half, for about 10 minutes. Mix in the basil.
3. Season the mahi-mahi with salt and pepper. Heat a grill skillet or grill pan over medium-high heat and coat with olive oil cooking spray. Add the fish and cook for 4 to 5 minutes per side. Serve topped with the artichoke caponata.

Nutrition: Calories: 246; Fats: 9.9 g; Carbohydrates: 13.1 g; Protein: 26.2 g

29
Grilled Fennel-Cumin Lamb Chops

10 minutes **30 minutes** **2**

Ingredients

- 1/4 teaspoon of salt
- 1 minced large garlic clove
- 1/8 teaspoon of cracked black pepper
- 3/4 teaspoon of crushed fennel seeds
- 1/4 teaspoon of ground coriander
- 4-6 sliced lamb rib chops
- 3/4 teaspoon of ground cumin

Directions

1. Trim fat from chops. Place the chops on a plate.
2. In a small bowl combine the garlic, fennel seeds, cumin, salt, coriander, and black pepper. Sprinkle the mixture evenly over chops; rub in with your fingers. Cover the chops with plastic wrap and marinate in the refrigerator for at least 30 minutes or up to 24 hours.
3. Grill chops on the rack of an uncovered grill directly over medium coals until chops are desired doneness.

Nutrition: Calories: 232; Carbohydrates: 1.2 g; Fats: 14.2 g; Protein: 24.9 g

30
Red Beans and Rice

15 minutes **45 minutes** **2**

Ingredients

- 1/2 cup of dry brown rice
- 1 cup of water, plus 1/4 cup
- 1 can of red beans, drained
- 1 tablespoon of ground cumin
- Juice of 1 lime
- 4 handfuls of fresh spinach
- Optional toppings: avocado, chopped tomatoes, Greek yogurt, onions

Directions

1. Mix rice plus water in a pot and bring to a boil. Cover and reduce heat to a low simmer. Cook for 30 to 40 minutes or according to package directions.
2. Meanwhile, add the beans, 1/4 cup of water, cumin, and lime juice to a medium skillet. Simmer for 5 to 7 minutes.
3. Once the liquid is mostly gone, remove it from the heat and add spinach. Cover and let spinach wilt slightly, 2 to 3 minutes. Mix in with the beans. Serve beans with rice. Add toppings, if using.

Nutrition: Calories: 232; Carbohydrates: 40.1 g; Fats: 1.5 g; Protein: 13.4 g

31
Chicken Tortillas

15 minutes — **5 minutes** — **4**

Ingredients

- 6 ounces of boneless, skinless, and cooked chicken breasts
- Black pepper
- 1/3 cup of fat-free yogurt
- 4 heated-up whole-wheat low-sodium tortillas
- 2 chopped tomatoes

Directions

1. Heat up a pan over medium heat, add one tortilla during those times, heat up, and hang them on the working surface. Spread yogurt on each tortilla, add chicken and tomatoes, roll, divide between plates and serve. Enjoy!

Nutrition: Calories: 206; Fats: 5.2 g; Carbohydrates: 25.8 g; Protein: 14.6 g

32
Hearty Lentil Soup

15 minutes — **30 minutes** — **4**

Ingredients

- 1 tablespoon of olive oil
- 2 carrots, peeled and chopped
- 2 celery stalks, diced
- 1 onion, chopped
- 1 teaspoon of dried thyme
- 1/2 teaspoon of garlic powder
- Freshly ground black pepper
- 1 (28-ounce) can of no-salt diced tomatoes, drained
- 1 cup of dry lentils
- 5 cups of water
- Salt

Directions

1. Heat up the oil in a large Dutch oven or pot over medium heat. Once the oil is simmering, add the carrot, celery, and onion. Cook, often stirring for 5 minutes.
2. Add the thyme, garlic powder, and black pepper. Cook for 30 seconds. Pour in the drained diced tomatoes and cook for a few more minutes, often stirring to enhance their flavor.
3. Put the lentils, water, plus a pinch of salt. Raise the heat and bring to a boil, then partially cover the pot and reduce heat to maintain a gentle simmer.
4. Cook for 30 minutes, or until lentils are tender but still hold their shape. Ladle into serving bowls and serve with a fresh green salad and whole-grain bread.

Nutrition: Calories: 170; Carbohydrates: 25.1 g; Fats: 3.4 g; Protein: 9.5 g

33
Black-Bean Soup

🥣 15 minutes   🕐 20 minutes   👥 4

Ingredients

- 1 yellow onion
- 1 tablespoon of olive oil
- 2 cans of black beans, drained
- 1 cup of diced fresh tomatoes
- 5 cups of low-sodium vegetable broth
- 1/4 teaspoon of freshly ground black pepper
- 1/4 cup of chopped fresh cilantro

Directions

1. Cook or sauté the onion in the olive oil for 4 to 5 minutes in a large saucepan over medium heat. Put the black beans, tomatoes, vegetable broth, and black pepper. Boil, then adjust heat to simmer for 15 minutes.
2. Remove, then work in batches, ladle the soup into a blender and process until somewhat smooth. Put it back into the pot, add the cilantro, and heat until warmed through. Serve immediately.

Nutrition: Calories: 209; Carbohydrates: 30.7 g; Fats: 3.5 g; Protein: 14.3 g

34
Chicken with Potatoes Olives & Sprouts

15 minutes

35 minutes

4

Ingredients

- 1 pound of chicken breasts, skinless, boneless, and cut into pieces
- 1/4 cup of olives, quartered
- 1 teaspoon of oregano
- 1 1/2 teaspoon of Dijon mustard
- 1 lemon juice
- 1/3 cup of vinaigrette dressing
- 1 medium onion, diced
- 3 cups of potatoes cut into pieces
- 4 cups of Brussels sprouts, trimmed and quartered
- 1/4 teaspoon of pepper
- 1/4 teaspoon of salt

Directions

1. Warm-up oven to 400°F. Place chicken in the center of the baking tray, then place potatoes, sprouts, and onions around the chicken.
2. In a small bowl, mix vinaigrette, oregano, mustard, lemon juice, and salt and pour over chicken and veggies. Sprinkle olives and season with pepper.
3. Bake in preheated oven for 20 minutes. Transfer chicken to a plate. Stir the vegetables and roast for 15 minutes more. Serve and enjoy.

Nutrition: Calories: 375; Fats: 11.3 g; Protein: 31.3 g; Carbohydrates: 37.4 g

35
Roasted Carrot Soup

15 minutes   **50 minutes**   **4**

Ingredients

- 8 large carrots, washed and peeled
- 6 tablespoons of olive oil
- 1-quart broth
- Cayenne pepper to taste
- Sunflower seeds and pepper to taste

Directions

1. Warm your oven to 425°F. Take a baking sheet, add carrots, drizzle olive oil, and roast for 30-45 minutes. Put roasted carrots into a blender and add broth, and puree. Pour into saucepan and heat soup. Season with sunflower seeds, pepper, and cayenne. Drizzle olive oil. Serve and enjoy!

Nutrition: Calories: 221; Fats: 15.8 g; Carbohydrates: 17.1 g; Protein: 3.5 g

36
Artichoke and Spinach Chicken

15 minutes   **5 minutes**   **4**

Ingredients

- 10 ounces of baby spinach
- 1/2 teaspoon of crushed red pepper flakes
- 14 ounces of chopped artichoke hearts
- 28 ounces of no-salt-added tomato sauce
- 2 tablespoons of essential olive oil
- 4 boneless and skinless chicken breasts

Directions

1. Heat up a pan with the oil over medium-high heat, add chicken and red pepper flakes and cook for 5 minutes on them. Add spinach, artichokes, and tomato sauce, toss, cook for ten minutes more, divide between plates and serve. Enjoy!

Nutrition: Calories: 312; Fats: 9.3 g; Carbohydrates: 21.6 g; Protein: 34.2 g

37
Eggplant Croquettes

15 minutes

5 minutes

2

Ingredients

- 1 eggplant, peeled, boiled
- 2 potatoes, mashed
- 2 tablespoons of almond meal
- 1 teaspoon of chili pepper
- 1 tablespoon of coconut oil
- 1 tablespoon of olive oil
- 1/4 teaspoon of ground nutmeg

Directions

2. Blend the eggplant until smooth.
3. Then mix it up with mashed potato, chili pepper, coconut oil, and ground nutmeg.
4. Make the croquettes from the eggplant mixture.
5. Heat up olive oil in the skillet.
6. Put the croquettes in the hot oil and cook them for 2 minutes per side or until they are light brown.

Nutrition: Calories: 256; Carbohydrates: 33.2 g; Fats: 11.8 g; Protein: 3.6 g

38
Stuffed Portobello

10 minutes

20 minutes

2

Ingredients

- 4 Portobello mushroom caps
- 1/2 zucchini, grated
- 1 tomato, diced
- 1 teaspoon of olive oil
- 1/2 teaspoon of dried parsley
- 1/4 teaspoon of minced garlic

Directions

1. In the mixing bowl, mix up diced tomato, grated zucchini, dried parsley, and minced garlic.
2. Fill the mushroom caps with zucchini mixture and transfer to the tray lined with baking paper.
3. Bake the vegetables for 20 minutes or until they are soft.

Nutrition: Calories: 86; Carbohydrates: 12.9 g; Fats: 2.6 g; Protein: 3.2 g

39
Spinach Casserole

5 minutes | **30 minutes** | **3**

Ingredients

- 2 cups of spinach, chopped
- 4 ounces of artichoke hearts, chopped
- 1/4 cup of low-fat yogurt
- 1 teaspoon of Italian seasonings
- 2 ounces of vegan mozzarella, shredded

Directions

1. Mix up all ingredients in the casserole mold and cover it with foil.
2. Then transfer it to the preheated 365°F oven and bake it for 30 minutes.

Nutrition: Calories: 112; Protein: 9.7 g; Carbohydrates: 9.3 g; Fats: 4.1 g

40
Tofu Turkey

15 minutes | **75 minutes** | **6**

Ingredients

- 1 onion, diced
- 1 cup of mushrooms, chopped
- 1 bell pepper, chopped
- 12 ounces of firm tofu, crumbled
- 1 teaspoon of dried rosemary
- 1 tablespoon of avocado oil
- 1/2 cup of marinara sauce
- 1 teaspoon of miso paste

Directions

1. Sauté onion, mushrooms, bell pepper, rosemary, miso paste, and avocado oil in the saucepan until the ingredients are cooked (appx.10-15 minutes).
2. Then put 1/2 part of the tofu in the round baking pan. Press well and make the medium whole in the center.
3. Put the mushroom mixture in the tofu whole and top it with marinara sauce.
4. Add remaining tofu and press it well. Cover the meal with foil.
5. Bake the tofu turkey for 60 minutes at 395°F.

Nutrition: Calories: 105; Protein: 9.9 g; Carbohydrates: 6.9 g; Fats: 4.1

41
Lemon and Cilantro Rice

 15 minutes   6 hours   4

Ingredients

- 3 cups of vegetable broth (low sodium)
- 1 1/2 cups of brown rice (uncooked)
- Juice of 2 lemons
- 2 tablespoons of chopped cilantro

Directions

1. In a slow cooker, place broth and rice. Cook on "low" for 5 hrs. Check the rice for doneness with a fork. Add the lemon juice and cilantro before serving.

Nutrition: Calories: 159; Carbohydrates: 31 g; Fats: 1.3 g; Protein: 4.8 g

42
Baby Spinach and Grains Mix

 10 minutes   4 hours   12

Ingredients

- 1 butternut squash, peeled and cubed
- 1 cup of the whole-grain blend, uncooked
- 12 ounces of low-sodium veggie stock
- 6 ounces of baby spinach
- 1 yellow onion, chopped
- 3 garlic cloves, minced
- 1/2 cup of water
- 2 teaspoons of thyme, chopped
- A pinch of black pepper

Directions

1. In your slow cooker, mix the squash with whole grain, onion, garlic, water, thyme, black pepper, stock, and spinach, cover, and cook on Low for 4 hours. Serve.

Nutrition: Calories: 63; Carbohydrates: 11.1 g; Fats: 0.9 g; Protein: 2.6 g

43
Quinoa Curry

15 minutes **4 hours** **8**

Ingredients

- 1 chopped sweet potato
- 2 cups of green beans
- 1/2 diced onion (white)
- 1 diced carrot
- 15 ounces of chickpeas (organic and drained)
- 28 ounces of tomatoes (diced)
- 29 ounces of coconut milk
- 2 minced garlic cloves
- 1/4 cup of quinoa
- 1 tablespoon of turmeric (ground)
- 1 tablespoon of ginger (grated)
- 1 1/2 cups of water
- 1 teaspoon of chili flakes
- 2 teaspoons of tamari sauce

Nutrition: Calories: 214; Carbohydrates: 32.9 g; Fats: 4.8 g; Protein: 9.9 g

Directions

1. Put all the listed fixing in the slow cooker. Add 1 cup of water. Stir well. Cook on "high" for 4 hrs. Serve with rice.

44
Vegetable Cheese Calzone

 15 minutes

 20 minutes

 4

Ingredients

- 3 asparagus stalks, cut into pieces
- 1/2 cup of spinach, chopped
- 1/2 cup of broccoli, chopped
- 1/2 cup of sliced mushrooms
- 2 tablespoons of garlic, minced
- 2 teaspoons of olive oil, divided
- 1/2 pound of frozen whole-wheat bread dough, thawed
- 1 medium tomato, sliced
- 1/2 cup of mozzarella, shredded
- 2/3 cup of pizza sauce

Directions

1. Prepare the oven to 400°F to preheat. Grease a baking sheet with cooking oil and set it aside. Toss asparagus with mushrooms, garlic, broccoli, and spinach in a bowl. Stir in 1 teaspoon of olive oil and mix well. Heat a greased skillet on medium heat.
2. Stir in vegetable mixture and sauté for 5 minutes. Put these vegetables aside. Cut the bread dough into quarters.
3. Spread each bread quarter on a floured surface into an oval. Add sautéed vegetables, 2 tablespoons of cheese, and a tomato slice to half of each oval.
4. Wet the edges of each oval and fold the dough over the vegetable filling. Pinch and press the two edges.
5. Put these calzones on the baking sheet. Brush each calzone with foil and bake for 10 minutes. Heat pizza sauce using a saucepan for a minute. Serve the calzone with pizza sauce.

Nutrition: Calories: 335; Fats: 11.3 g; Carbohydrates: 45.5 g; Protein: 13.1 g

45
Loaded Baked Sweet Potatoes

15 minutes | 20 minutes | 4

Ingredients

- 4 sweet potatoes
- 1/2 cup of nonfat or low-fat plain Greek yogurt
- Freshly ground black pepper
- 1 teaspoon of olive oil
- 1 red bell pepper, cored and diced
- 1/2 red onion, diced
- 1 teaspoon of ground cumin
- 1 (15-ounce) can of chickpeas, drained and rinsed

Directions

1. Prick the potatoes using a fork and cook on your microwave's potato setting until potatoes are soft and cooked through, about 8 to 10 minutes for 4 potatoes. If you don't have a microwave, bake at 400°F for about 45 minutes.
2. Combine the yogurt and black pepper in a small bowl and mix well. Heat the oil in a medium pot over medium heat. Add bell pepper, onion, cumin, and additional black pepper to taste.
3. Add the chickpeas, stir to combine, and heat for about 5 minutes. Slice the potatoes lengthwise down the middle and top each half with a portion of the bean mixture followed by 1 to 2 tablespoons of the yogurt. Serve immediately.

Nutrition: Calories: 328; Fats: 2.1 g; Carbohydrate: 61.4 g; Protein: 15.3 g

46
White Beans with Spinach and Pan-Roasted Tomatoes

15 minutes

10 minutes

2

Ingredients

- 1 tablespoon of olive oil
- 4 small plum tomatoes, halved lengthwise
- 10 ounces of frozen spinach, defrosted and squeezed of excess water
- 2 garlic cloves, thinly sliced
- 2 tablespoons of water
- 1/4 teaspoon of freshly ground black pepper
- 1 can of white beans, drained
- Juice of 1 lemon

Directions

1. Heat up the oil in a large skillet over medium-high heat. Put the tomatoes, cut side down, and cook for 3 to 5 minutes; turn and cook for 1 minute more. Transfer to a plate.
2. Reduce heat to medium and add the spinach, garlic, water, and pepper to the skillet. Cook, tossing until the spinach is heated through, 2 to 3 minutes.
3. Return the tomatoes to the skillet, put the white beans and lemon juice, and toss until heated through 1 to 2 minutes.

Nutrition: Calories: 248; Carbohydrates: 33.1 g; Fats: 6.3 g; Protein: 15.5 g

47
Butternut-Squash Macaroni and Cheese

15 minutes   20 minutes   2

Ingredients

- 1 cup of whole-wheat ziti macaroni
- 2 cups of peeled, and cubed butternut squash
- 1 cup of nonfat or low-fat milk, divided
- Freshly ground black pepper
- 1 teaspoon of Dijon mustard
- 1 tablespoon of olive oil
- 1/4 cup of shredded low-fat cheddar cheese

Directions

1. Cook the pasta al dente. Put the butternut squash plus 1/2 cup of milk in a medium saucepan and place over medium-high heat. Season with black pepper. Bring it to a simmer. Lower the heat, then cook until fork-tender, 8 to 10 minutes.
2. To a blender, add squash and Dijon mustard. Purée until smooth. Meanwhile, place a large sauté pan over medium heat and add olive oil. Add the squash purée and the remaining 1/2 cup of milk. Simmer for 5 minutes. Add the cheese and stir to combine.
3. Add the pasta to the sauté pan and stir to combine. Serve immediately.

Nutrition: Calories: 394; Carbohydrates: 60.9 g; Fats: 8.5 g; Protein: 18.5 g

48
Pasta with Tomatoes and Peas

 15 minutes   15 minutes   2

Ingredients

- 1/2 cup of whole-grain pasta of choice
- 8 cups of water, plus 1/4 for finishing
- 1 cup of frozen peas
- 1 tablespoon of olive oil
- 1 cup of cherry tomatoes, halved
- 1/4 teaspoon of freshly ground black pepper
- 1 teaspoon of dried basil
- 1/4 cup of grated Parmesan cheese (low sodium)

Directions

1. Cook the pasta al dente. Add the water to the same pot you used to cook the pasta, and when it's boiling, add the peas. Cook for 5 minutes. Drain and set it aside.
2. Heat up the oil in a large skillet over medium heat. Add the cherry tomatoes, put a lid on the skillet and let the tomatoes soften for about 5 minutes, stirring a few times.
3. Season with black pepper and basil. Toss in the pasta, peas, and 1/4 cup of water, stir and remove from the heat. Serve topped with Parmesan.

Nutrition: Calories: 326; Carbohydrates: 44.7 g; Fats: 10.2 g; Protein: 13.8 g

49
Poached Salmon with Creamy Piccata Sauce

 5 minutes   15 minutes   4

Ingredients

- 1 pound of center-cut salmon fillet skinned and cut into 4 portions
- 2 tablespoons of lemon juice
- 2 teaspoons of extra-virgin olive oil
- 1/4 cup of reduced-fat sour cream
- 1 large shallot, minced
- 1 cup of dry white wine, divided
- 1 tablespoon of chopped fresh dill
- 4 teaspoons of capers, rinsed
- 1/4 teaspoon of salt

Directions

1. Place salmon in a wide skillet and add 1/2 cup of wine and sufficient water to cover the salmon. Bring it to a boil over high-temperature heat. Simmer, turn the salmon over, cook for 5 minutes and then remove from the heat.
2. In the meantime, heat up oil in a medium skillet over moderate heat. Add shallot and cook, stirring, until scented, about 30 seconds. Add the remaining 1/2 cup of wine; boil until slightly condensed, about 1 minute.
3. Stir in lemon juice plus capers; cook 1 minute more. Remove and stir in sour cream and salt. Top the salmon with the sauce and relish it with dill before serving.

Nutrition: Calories: 342; Fats: 22.3 g; Carbohydrates: 3.7 g; Protein: 31.3 g

50
Healthy Vegetable Fried Rice

 15 minutes 10 minutes 4

Ingredients

For the sauce:

- 1/3 cup of garlic vinegar
- 1 1/2 tablespoons of dark molasses
- 1 teaspoon of onion powder

For the fried rice:

- 1 teaspoon of olive oil
- 2 lightly beaten whole eggs + 4 egg whites
- 1 cup of frozen mixed vegetables
- 1 cup of frozen edamame
- 2 cups of cooked brown rice

Directions

1. Prepare the sauce by combining the garlic vinegar, molasses, and onion powder in a glass jar. Shake well.
2. Heat up oil in a large wok or skillet over medium-high heat. Add eggs and egg whites, and let cook until the eggs set, for about 1 minute.
3. Break up eggs with a spatula or spoon into small pieces. Add frozen mixed vegetables and frozen edamame. Cook for 4 minutes, stirring frequently.
4. Add the brown rice and sauce to the vegetable-and-egg mixture. Cook for 5 minutes or until heated through. Serve immediately.

Nutrition: Calories: 293; Carbohydrates: 42.5 g; Fats: 6.6 g; Protein: 16.3 g

51
Cheesy Cauliflower Fritters

10 minutes   7 minutes   3

Ingredients

- 1/2 cup of chopped parsley
- 1 cup of Italian breadcrumbs
- 1/3 cup of shredded mozzarella cheese
- 1/3 cup of shredded sharp cheddar cheese
- One egg
- Two minced garlic cloves
- Three chopped scallions
- One head of cauliflower

Directions

1. Cut the cauliflower up into florets. Wash well and pat dry. Place into a food processor and pulse 20-30 seconds till it looks like rice.
2. Place the cauliflower rice in a bowl and mix with pepper, salt, egg, cheeses, breadcrumbs, garlic, and scallions.
3. With hands, form 15 patties of the mixture, and then add more breadcrumbs if needed.
4. With olive oil, spritz patties, and put the fitters into your Instant Crisp Air Fryer. Pile it in a single layer. Lock the air fryer lid. Set temperature to 390°F, and set time to 7 minutes, flipping after 7 minutes.

Nutrition: Calories: 243; Fats: 12.3 g; Protein: 13.6 g; Carbohydrates: 19.5 g

52
Zucchini Parmesan Chips

10 minutes   8 minutes   2

Ingredients

- 1/2 tsp. paprika
- 1/2 cup of grated parmesan cheese
- 1/2 cup of Italian breadcrumbs
- One lightly beaten egg
- Two thinly sliced zucchinis

Directions

1. Use a very sharp knife or mandolin slicer to slice the zucchini as thinly as you can. Pat off extra moisture.
2. Beat the egg with a pinch of pepper and salt and a bit of water.
3. Combine paprika, cheese, and breadcrumbs in a bowl.
4. Dip slices of zucchini into the egg mixture and then into breadcrumb mixture. Press gently to coat.
5. With olive oil cooking spray, mist encrusted zucchini slices. Put into your Instant Crisp Air Fryer in a single layer. Latch the air fryer lid. Set temperature to 350°F and set time to 8 minutes.
6. Sprinkle with salt and serve with salsa.

Nutrition: Calories: 198; Fats: 6.5 g; Protein: 10.1 g; Carbohydrates: 24.5 g

53
Jalapeno Cheese Balls

10 minutes	8 minutes	2

Ingredients

- 1-ounce cream cheese
- 1/6 cup shredded mozzarella cheese
- 1/6 cup shredded Cheddar cheese
- 1/2 jalapeños, finely chopped
- 1/2 cup breadcrumbs
- Two eggs
- 1/2 cup all-purpose flour
- Pepper
- Mixed herbs
- Cooking oil

Directions

1. Combine the cream cheese, mozzarella, Cheddar, and jalapeños in a medium bowl. Mix well.
2. Form the cheese mixture into balls about an inch thick. You may also use a small ice cream scoop. It works well.
3. Arrange the cheese balls on a sheet pan and place in the freezer for 15 minutes. It will help the cheese balls maintain their shape while frying.
4. Spray the Instant Crisp Air Fryer basket with cooking oil.
5. Place the breadcrumbs in a small bowl. In another small bowl, beat the eggs. In the third small bowl, combine the flour with mixed herbs and pepper to taste, and mix well.
6. Remove the cheese balls from the freezer. Plunge the cheese balls in the flour, then the eggs, and then the breadcrumbs.
7. Place the cheese balls in the Instant Crisp Air Fryer. Spray with cooking oil. Lock the air fryer lid. Cook for 8 minutes.
8. Open the Instant Crisp Air Fryer and flip the cheese balls. I recommend flipping them instead of shaking, so the balls maintain their form. Cook an additional 4 minutes.
9. Cool before serving.

Nutrition: Calories: 334; Fats: 10.6 g; Protein: 17.4 g; Carbohydrates: 42.3 g

54
Crispy Roasted Broccoli

10 minutes	8 minutes	1

Ingredients

- 1/4 tsp. Masala
- 1/2 tsp. red chili powder
- 1/2 tsp. salt
- 1/4 tsp. turmeric powder
- 1 tbsp. chickpea flour
- 1 tbsp. yogurt
- 1/2-pound broccoli

Directions

1. Cut broccoli up into florets. Immerse in a bowl of water with two teaspoons of salt for at least half an hour to remove impurities.
2. Take out broccoli florets from water and let drain. Wipe down thoroughly.
3. Mix all other ingredients to create a marinade.
4. Toss broccoli florets in the marinade. Cover and chill 15-30 minutes.
5. Preheat the Instant Crisp Air Fryer to 390 degrees. Place marinated broccoli florets into the fryer, lock the air fryer lid, set the temperature to 350°F, and set time to 10 minutes. Florets will be crispy when done.

Nutrition: Calories: 97; Fats: 3.3 g; Protein: 7.7 g; Carbohydrates: 8.5 g

55
Coconut Battered Cauliflower Bites

5 minutes   **20 minutes**   **2**

Ingredients

- Salt and pepper to taste
- One flax egg or one tablespoon flaxseed meal + 3 tablespoon water
- One small cauliflower, cut into florets
- One teaspoon mixed spice
- 1/2 teaspoon mustard powder
- Two tablespoons maple syrup
- One clove of garlic, minced
- Two tablespoons soy sauce
- 1/3 cup oats flour
- 1/3 cup plain flour
- 1/3 cup desiccated coconut

Directions

1. In a mixing bowl, mix oats, flour, and desiccated coconut. Season with salt and pepper to taste. Set aside.
2. In another bowl, place the flax egg and add a pinch of salt to taste. Set aside.
3. Season the cauliflower with mixed spice and mustard powder.
4. Dredge the florets in the flax egg first, then in the flour mixture.
5. Place it inside the Instant Crisp Air Fryer, lock the air fryer lid, and cook at 400°F or 15 minutes.
6. Meanwhile, place the maple syrup, garlic, and soy sauce in a saucepan and heat over medium flame. Wait for it to boil and adjust the heat to low until the sauce thickens.
7. After 15 minutes, take out the Instant Crisp Air Fryer's florets and place them in the saucepan.
8. Toss to coat the florets and place inside the Instant Crisp Air Fryer and cook for another 5 minutes.

Nutrition: Calories: 296; Fats: 8.3 g; Protein: 11.9 g; Carbohydrates: 43.1 g

chapter 3

DINNER RECIPES

56
Portobello-Mushroom Cheeseburgers

15 minutes

10 minutes

4

Ingredients

- 4 Portobello mushrooms, caps removed and brushed clean
- 1 tablespoon of olive oil
- 1/2 teaspoon of freshly ground black pepper
- 1 tablespoon of red wine vinegar
- 4 slices of reduced-fat Swiss cheese, sliced thin
- 4 whole-wheat 100-calorie sandwiches thins
- 1/2 avocado, sliced thin

Directions

1. Heat up a skillet or grill pan over medium-high heat. Clean the mushrooms and remove the stems. Brush each cap with olive oil and sprinkle with black pepper. Place in skillet cap-side up and cook for about 4 minutes. Flip and cook for another 4 minutes.
2. Sprinkle with the red wine vinegar and flip. Add the cheese and cook for 2 more minutes. For optimal melting, place a lid loosely over the pan. Meanwhile, toast the sandwich thins. Create your burgers by topping each with sliced avocado. Enjoy immediately.

Nutrition: Calories: 280; Fats: 11.3 g; Carbohydrate: 26.3 g; Protein: 17.9 g

57
Chilled Cucumber and Avocado Soup with Dill

15 minutes   30 minutes   4

Ingredients

- 2 English cucumbers, peeled and diced, plus 1/4 cup of reserved for garnish
- 1 avocado, peeled, pitted, and chopped, plus 1/4 cup of reserved for garnish
- 1 1/2 cups of nonfat or low-fat plain Greek yogurt
- 1/2 cup of cold water
- 1/3 cup of loosely packed dill, plus sprigs for garnish
- 1 tablespoon of freshly squeezed lemon juice
- 1/4 teaspoon of freshly ground black pepper
- 1/4 teaspoon of salt
- 1 garlic clove

Directions

1. Purée ingredients in a blender until smooth. If you prefer a thinner soup, add more water until you reach the desired consistency. Divide soup among 4 bowls. Cover with plastic wrap and refrigerate for 30 minutes. Garnish with cucumber, avocado, and dill sprigs, if desired.

Nutrition: Calories: 124; Fats: 8.7 g; Carbohydrate: 4.8 g; Protein: 6.5 g

58
Cauliflower Mashed Potatoes

10 minutes   10 minutes   4

Ingredients

- 16 cups of water (enough to cover cauliflower)
- 1 head cauliflower (about 3 pounds), trimmed and cut into florets
- 4 garlic cloves
- 1 tablespoon of olive oil
- 1/4 teaspoon of salt
- 1/8 teaspoon of freshly ground black pepper
- 2 teaspoons of dried parsley

Directions

2. Boil a large pot of water, then the cauliflower and garlic. Cook for 10 minutes, then strain. Move it back to the hot pan, and let it stand for 2 to 3 minutes with the lid on.
3. Put the cauliflower plus garlic in a food processor or blender. Add the olive oil, salt, pepper, and purée until smooth. Taste and adjust the salt and pepper.
4. Remove, then put the parsley, and mix until combined. Garnish with additional olive oil, if desired. Serve immediately.

Nutrition: Calories: 67 g; Fats: 2.4 g; Carbohydrate: 8.4 g; Protein: 2.8 g

59
Broccoli with Garlic and Lemon

2 minutes   4 minutes   4

Ingredients

- 1 cup of water
- 4 cups of broccoli florets
- 1 teaspoon of olive oil
- 1 tablespoon of minced garlic
- 1 teaspoon of lemon zest
- Salt
- Freshly ground black pepper

Directions

1. Put the broccoli in the boiling water in a small saucepan and cook for 2 to 3 minutes. The broccoli should retain its bright-green color. Drain the water from the broccoli.
2. Put the olive oil in a small sauté pan over medium-high heat. Add the garlic and sauté for 30 seconds. Put the broccoli, lemon zest, salt, plus pepper. Combine well and serve.

Nutrition: Calories: 74 g; Fats: 2.5 g; Carbohydrate: 9.1 g; Protein: 3.7 g

60
Brown Rice Pilaf

5 minutes   **10 minutes**   **4**

Ingredients

- 1 cup of low-sodium vegetable broth
- 1/2 tablespoon of olive oil
- 1 garlic clove, minced
- 1 scallion, thinly sliced
- 1 tablespoon of minced onion flakes
- 1 cup of instant brown rice
- 1/8 teaspoon of freshly ground black pepper

Directions

1. Mix the vegetable broth, olive oil, garlic, scallion, and minced onion flakes in a saucepan and boil. Put rice, then boil it again, adjust the heat and simmer for 10 minutes. Remove and let stand for 5 minutes. Fluff with a fork and season with black pepper.

Nutrition: Calories: 158 g; Fats: 1.8 g; Carbohydrate: 27.9 g; Protein: 7.2 g

61
Sweet Potatoes and Apples

15 minutes   **40 minutes**   **4**

Ingredients

- 2 sweet potatoes, sliced into 1" cubes
- 2 apples, cut into 1" cubes
- 3 tablespoons of extra virgin olive oil, divided
- 1/4 teaspoon of black pepper, ground
- 1 teaspoon of cinnamon, ground
- 2 tablespoons of maple syrup

Directions

1. Warm the oven to 425°F and grease a large baking sheet with non-stick cooking spray. Toss the cubed sweet potatoes with two tablespoons of olive oil and black pepper until coated. Roast the potatoes for twenty minutes, stirring them once halfway through the process.
2. Meanwhile, toss the apples with the remaining tablespoon of olive oil, cinnamon, and maple syrup until evenly coated. After the sweet potatoes have cooked for twenty minutes, add the apples to the baking sheet and toss the sweet potatoes and apples.
3. Return to the oven, then roast it for twenty more minutes, once again giving it a good stir halfway through. Once the potatoes and apples are caramelized from the maple syrup, remove them from the oven and serve hot.

Nutrition: Calories: 187; Carbohydrates: 28.8 g; Fats: 7.5 g; Protein: 1.2 g

62
Chicken & Rice Soup

15 minutes   8 hours   6

Ingredients

- 1 pound of boneless, skinless chicken thighs, cut into 1-inch pieces
- 1 onion, chopped
- 3 carrots, peeled and sliced
- 2 celery stalks, sliced
- 6 cups of low-sodium Poultry Broth or store-bought
- 1 teaspoon of garlic powder
- 1 teaspoon of dried rosemary
- 1/4 teaspoon of sea salt
- 1/4 teaspoon of freshly ground black pepper
- 3 cups of cooked Brown Rice

Directions

1. In your slow cooker, combine the chicken, onion, carrots, celery, broth, garlic powder, rosemary, salt, and pepper. Cover and cook on Low for 8 hours. Stir in the rice about 10 minutes before serving, and allow the broth to warm it.

Nutrition: Calories: 311; Fats: 7.5 g; Carbohydrates: 36.7 g; Protein: 24.2 g

63
Chicken Corn Chowder

15 minutes   8 hours   6

Ingredients

- 1 pound of boneless, skinless chicken thighs, cut into 1-inch pieces
- 2 onions, chopped
- 3 jalapeño peppers, seeded and minced
- 2 red bell peppers, seeded and chopped
- 1 1/2 cups of fresh or frozen corn
- 6 cups of low-sodium Poultry Broth or store-bought
- 1 teaspoon of garlic powder
- 1/2 teaspoon of sea salt
- 1/4 teaspoon of freshly ground black pepper
- 1 cup of skim milk

Directions

1. In your slow cooker, combine the chicken, onions, jalapeños, red bell peppers, corn, broth, garlic powder, salt, and pepper. Cover and cook on Low for 8 hours. Stir in the skim milk just before serving.

Nutrition: Calories: 297; Fats: 8.6 g; Carbohydrates: 30.3 g; Protein: 25.1 g

64
Turkey Ginger Soup

 15 minutes

 8 hours

 6

Ingredients

- 1 pound of boneless, skinless turkey thighs, cut into 1-inch pieces
- 1 pound of fresh shiitake mushrooms halved
- 3 carrots, peeled and sliced
- 2 cups of frozen peas
- 1 tablespoon of grated fresh ginger
- 6 cups of low-sodium Poultry Broth or store-bought
- 1 tablespoon of low-sodium soy sauce
- 1 teaspoon of toasted sesame oil
- 2 teaspoons of garlic powder
- 1 1/2 cups of cooked Brown Rice

Directions

1. In your slow cooker, combine the turkey, mushrooms, carrots, peas, ginger, broth, soy sauce, sesame oil, and garlic powder. Cover and cook on Low for 8 hours. About 30 minutes before serving, stir in the rice to warm it through.

Nutrition: Calories: 325; Fats: 8.3 g; Carbohydrates: 35.8 g; Protein: 26.7 g

65
Spanish Rice

15 minutes   1 hour & 35 minutes   8

Ingredients

- 2 cups of brown rice
- 1/4 cup of extra virgin olive oil
- 2 garlic cloves, minced
- 1 onion, diced
- 2 tomatoes, diced
- 1 jalapeno, seeded and diced
- 1 tablespoon of tomato paste
- 1/2 cup of cilantro, chopped
- 2 1/2 cups of chicken broth, low sodium

Directions

1. Warm the oven to 375°F. Puree the tomatoes, onion, plus garlic using a blender or food processor. Measure out two cups of this vegetable puree to use and discard the excess.
2. Into a large oven-safe Dutch pan, heat the extra virgin olive oil over medium heat until hot and shimmering. Add in the jalapeno and rice to toast, cooking while occasionally stirring for two to three minutes.
3. Slowly stir the chicken broth into the rice, followed by the vegetable puree and tomato paste. Stir until combined and increase the heat to medium-high until the broth reaches a boil.
4. Cover the Dutch pan with an oven-safe lid, transfer the pot to the preheated oven, and bake for 1 hour and 15 minutes. Remove and stir the cilantro into the rice. Serve.

Nutrition: Calories: 182; Carbohydrates: 29.4 g; Fats: 5.2 g; Protein: 4.6 g

66
Roasted Turnips

15 minutes   30 minutes   4

Ingredients

- 2 cups of turnips, peels, and cut into 1/2" cubes
- 1/4 teaspoon of black pepper, ground
- 1/2 teaspoon of garlic powder
- 1/2 teaspoon of onion powder
- 1 tablespoon of extra virgin olive oil

Directions

1. Warm the oven to 400°F and prepare a large baking sheet, setting it aside. Begin by trimming the top and bottom edges off of the turnips and peeling them if you wish. Slice them into 1/2-inch cubes.
2. Toss the turnips with the extra virgin olive oil and seasonings and then spread them out on the prepared baking sheet. Roast the turnips until tender, stirring them halfway through, about thirty minutes in total.

Nutrition: Calories: 68; Carbohydrates: 8.5 g; Fats: 2.9 g; Protein: 2.3 g

67
Crab, Zucchini, and Watermelon Soup

4 hours

0 minutes

4

Ingredients

- 1/4 cup of basil, chopped
- 2 pounds of tomatoes
- 5 cups of watermelon, cubed
- 1/4 cup of red wine vinegar
- 1/3 cup of olive oil
- 2 garlic cloves, minced
- 1 zucchini, chopped
- Black pepper to the taste
- 1 cup of crabmeat

Directions

1. In your food processor, mix tomatoes with basil, vinegar, 4 cups of watermelon, garlic, 1/3 cup of oil, and black pepper to the taste, pulse, pour into a bowl and keep in the fridge for 1 hour.
2. Divide this into bowls, add zucchini, crab, and the rest of the watermelon and serve.
3. Enjoy!

Nutrition: Calories: 184; Fats: 9.3 g; Carbohydrates: 16.8 g; Protein: 8.7 g

68
Jerk Beef and Plantain Kabobs

10 minutes

15 minutes

4

Ingredients

- 2 peeled and sliced ripe plantains
- 2 tablespoons of red wine vinegar
- Lime wedges
- 1 tablespoon of cooking oil
- 1 sliced medium red onion
- 12 ounces of sliced boneless beef sirloin steak
- 1 tablespoon of Jamaican jerk seasoning

Directions

1. Trim fat from meat. Cut into 1-inch pieces. In a small bowl, stir together red wine vinegar, oil, and jerk seasoning. Toss meat cubes with half of the vinegar mixture. On long skewers, alternately thread meat, plantain chunks, and onion wedges, leaving a 1/4-inch space between pieces.
2. Brush plantains and onion wedges with the remaining vinegar mixture.
3. Place skewers on the rack of an uncovered grill directly over medium coals. Grill for 12 to 15 minutes or until meat is desired doneness, turning occasionally.
4. Serve with lime wedges.

Nutrition: Calories: 269; Fats: 15.7 g; Carbohydrates: 9.8 g; Protein: 22.1 g

69
Herbed Seafood Casserole

15 minutes   **50 minutes**   **12**

Ingredients

- 1 1/2 cups of uncooked long-grain rice
- 2 tablespoons of butter
- 1/4 teaspoon of pepper
- 2 tablespoons of minced fresh parsley
- 1 medium onion, finely chopped
- 3 garlic cloves, minced
- 1 medium carrot, shredded
- 1/2 teaspoon of salt
- 3 celery ribs, thinly sliced
- 1 1/2 teaspoon of snipped fresh dill or 1/2 teaspoon of dill weed

SEAFOOD:
- 1 pound of uncooked medium shrimp, peeled, and deveined
- 1 can of crab meat, drained, flaked, and cartilage removed
- 1/4 cup of all-purpose flour
- 1 pound of bay scallops
- 1/2 teaspoon of salt
- 1 package (8 ounces) cream cheese, cubed
- 5 tablespoons of butter, cubed
- 1 1/2 cups of half-and-half cream
- 1 1/2 teaspoon of snipped fresh dill or 1/2 teaspoon of dill weed
- 1/4 teaspoon of dried thyme
- 1/4 teaspoon of pepper

TOPPING:
- 2 tablespoons of butter, melted
- 1 1/2 cups of soft breadcrumbs

Directions

1. Preheat the oven to 325°F. Cook rice according to package directions. In the meantime, in a big skillet, heat butter over moderate heat. Add onion, celery, and carrot; cook and stir until crisp-tender. Add garlic, pepper, and salt; cook 1 minute longer. Add to the cooked rice. Stir in parsley and dill. Transfer to a greased baking dish.
2. Fill a large saucepan with 2/3 full of water and bring to a boil. Reduce heat to medium. Add shrimp; simmer, uncovered, for 30 seconds. Add scallops; simmer for 3 minutes or just until shrimp turn pink, and scallops are firm and dense. Reserve 1 cup of cooking liquid. Put the seafood in a large bowl; stir in crab.
3. Dissolve the butter over medium heat in a small saucepan. Stir in flour until mixed; slowly stir in cream and kept cooking liquid. Boil for 2 minutes or until condensed and foamy. Reduce heat. Stir in cream cheese, dill and season until smooth. Stir into the seafood blend.
4. Pour over the rice mixture. Mix the breadcrumbs with melted butter; sprinkle over the top. Bake, uncovered, for 50 minutes or until it turns golden brown. Stand 10 minutes before dishing.

Nutrition: Calories: 342; Fats: 16.4 g; Carbohydrate: 22.9 g; Protein: 25.8 g

70
Lemon Herb Baked Salmon

15 minutes   **20 minutes**   **8**

Ingredients

- 3-4 pound of salmon (cut into 4 6-ounce fillets)
- Salt & pepper
- 1 lemon divided
- 2 tablespoons of butter melted

Topping:

- 3/4 cup of Panko breadcrumbs
- 3 tablespoons of butter melted
- 2 tablespoons of parmesan cheese shredded
- 1 tablespoon of fresh dill minced
- Zest from one lemon
- 2 tablespoons of fresh parsley minced
- 3 garlic cloves minced

Directions

1. Preheat the oven to 400°F. Put all ingredients in a small bowl. Streak a pan with foil and spray with cooking spray. Put salmon on the pan and brush with melted butter.
2. Season with salt and pepper and crush 1/2 of the lemon over the top. Sprinkle crumb mixture over salmon. Bake exposed for 15 minutes or until salmon flakes easily and is cooked.

Nutrition: Calories: 453; Carbohydrates: 7.5 g; Protein: 45.4 g; Fats: 26.9 g

71
Beef with Cucumber Raito

 10 minutes   30 minutes   2

Ingredients

- 1/2 teaspoon of lemon-pepper seasoning
- 1/4 cup of coarsely shredded unpeeled cucumber
- Black pepper to taste
- 1 tablespoon of finely chopped red onion
- 1/4 teaspoon of sugar
- 1 pound of sliced de-boned beef sirloin steak
- 8 ounces of plain fat-free yogurt
- 1 tablespoon of snipped fresh mint

Directions

1. Preheat broiler.
2. Using a small bowl mix yogurt, cucumber, onion, snipped mint, and sugar. Season to taste with pepper; put it aside
3. Trim fat from meat. Sprinkle meat using lemon-pepper seasoning.
4. Plut meat on the unheated rack of a broiler pan. Broil 3 to 4 inches from heat, turning meat over after half of the broiling time.
5. Allow 15 to 17 minutes for medium-rare (145°F) and 20 to 22 minutes for medium (160°F).
6. Cut steak across the grain to form thin slices.
7. Serve and enjoy.

Nutrition: Calories: 424; Fats: 23.1 g; Carbohydrates: 7.5 g; Protein: 46.8 g

72
Rustic Beef and Barley Soup

10 Minutes   40 minutes   6

Ingredients

- 1 teaspoon of olive oil
- 1 pound of beef round steak, sliced into strips
- 2 cups of yellow onion, chopped
- 1 cup of diced celery
- 4 garlic cloves, chopped
- 1 cup of diced Roma tomatoes
- 1/2 cup of diced sweet potato
- 1/2 cup of diced mushrooms
- 1 cup of diced carrots
- 1/4 cup of uncooked barley
- 3 cups of low sodium vegetable stock
- 1 teaspoon of dried sage
- 1 paprika
- A dash of black pepper to taste
- 1 cup of chopped kale

Directions

1. In a large pot, heat the oil over medium flame and stir in the beef. Cook for 5 minutes while stirring constantly until all sides turn brown.
2. Stir in the onion, celery, and garlic until fragrant.
3. Add in the rest of the ingredients except for the kale.
4. Bring to a boil and cook for 30 minutes until everything is tender.
5. Stir in the kale last and cook for another 5 minutes.

Nutrition: Calories: 251; Protein: 19.2 g; Carbohydrates: 22.3 g; Fats: 9.4 g

73
Asian Pork Tenderloin

10 Minutes　　　　**15 minutes**　　　　**4**

Ingredients

- 2 tablespoons of sesame seeds
- 1 teaspoon of ground coriander
- 1/8 teaspoon of cayenne pepper
- 1/8 teaspoon of celery seed
- 1/2 teaspoon of minced onion
- 1/4 teaspoon of ground cumin
- 1/8 teaspoon of ground cinnamon
- 1 tablespoon of sesame oil
- 1 pound of pork tenderloin sliced into 4 equal portions

Directions

1. Preheat the oven to 400°F.
2. In a skillet, toast the sesame seeds over low heat and set them aside. Allow the sesame seeds to cool.
3. In a bowl, combine the rest of the ingredients except for the pork tenderloin. Stir in the toasted sesame seeds.
4. Place the pork tenderloin in a baking dish and rub the spices on both sides.
5. Place the baking dish with the pork in the oven and bake for 15 minutes or until the internal temperature of the meat reaches 170°F.
6. Serve warm.

Nutrition: Calories: 246; Protein: 26.8 g; Carbohydrates: 0.9 g; Fats: 15.2 g

74
Simple Beef Brisket and Tomato Soup

10 Minutes

3 hours

8

Ingredients

- 1 tablespoon of olive oil
- 2 1/2 pounds of beef brisket, trimmed of fat and cut into 8 equal parts
- A dash of ground black pepper
- 1 1/2 cups of chopped onions
- 4 garlic cloves, smashed
- 1 teaspoon of dried thyme
- 1 cup of ripe Roma tomatoes, chopped
- 1/4 cup of red wine vinegar
- 1 cup of beef stock, low sodium, or homemade

Directions

1. In a heavy pot, heat the oil over medium-high heat.
2. Season the brisket with ground black pepper and place in the pot.
3. Cook while stirring constantly until the beef turns brown on all sides.
4. Stir in the onions and cook until fragrant. Add in the garlic and thyme and cook for another minute until fragrant.
5. Pour in the rest of the ingredients and bring to a boil.
6. Cook until the beef is tender. This may take about 3 hours or more.

Nutrition: Calories: 273; Protein: 31.8 g; Carbohydrates: 5.6 g; Fats: 13.9 g

75
Beef Stew with Fennel and Shallots

10 Minutes   40 minutes   6

Ingredients

- 1 tablespoon of olive oil
- 1 pound of boneless lean beef stew meat, trimmed from fat and cut into cubes
- 1/2 fennel bulb, trimmed and sliced thinly
- 3 large shallots, chopped
- 3/4 teaspoons of ground black pepper
- 2 fresh thyme sprigs
- 1 bay leaf
- 3 cups of low sodium beef broth
- 1/2 cup of red wine
- 4 large carrots, peeled, and cut into chunks
- 4 large white potatoes, peeled, and cut into chunks
- 3 portobello mushrooms, cleaned, and cut into chunks
- 1/3 cup of Italian parsley, chopped

Directions

1. Heat oil in a pot over medium heat and stir in the beef cubes for 5 minutes or until all sides turn brown.
2. Stir in the fennel, shallots, black pepper, and thyme for one minute or until the ingredients become fragrant.
3. Stir in the bay leaf, broth, red wine, carrots, white potatoes, and mushrooms.
4. Bring to a boil and cook for 30 minutes or until everything is tender.
5. Stir in the parsley last.

Nutrition: Calories: 250; Protein: 17.3 g; Carbohydrates: 25.6 g; Fats: 8.8 g

76
Zucchini Tomato Bake

15 minutes   **30 minutes**   **4**

Ingredients

- 10 ounces of grape tomatoes, cut in half
- 2 zucchinis
- 5 garlic cloves, minced
- 1 teaspoon of Italian herb seasoning
- 1/4 teaspoon of black pepper, ground
- 1/3 cup of parsley, fresh, chopped
- 1/2 cup of parmesan cheese, low sodium, grated

Directions

1. Warm the oven to 350°F and coat a large baking sheet with non-stick cooking spray. Mix the tomatoes, zucchini, garlic, Italian herb seasoning, Black pepper, and Parmesan cheese in a bowl.
2. Put the mixture out on the baking sheet and roast for thirty minutes. Remove, and garnish with parsley over the top before serving.

Nutrition: Calories: 125; Carbohydrates: 9.4 g; Fats: 6.2 g; Protein: 7.2 g

77
Beef Pot

10 minutes   **40 minutes**   **2**

Ingredients

- 4 tablespoons of sour cream
- 1/4 shredded cabbage head
- 1 teaspoon of butter
- 2 peeled, and sliced carrots
- 1 chopped onion
- 10 ounces of boiled and sliced beef tenderloin
- 1 tablespoon of flour

Directions

1. Sauté the cabbage, carrots, and onions in butter.
2. Spray a pot with cooking spray.
3. In layers place the sautéed vegetables, then beef, then another layer of vegetables.
4. Beat the sour cream with flour until smooth and pour over the beef.
5. Cover and bake at 400°F for 40 minutes.

Nutrition: Calories: 416; Carbohydrates: 17.4 g; Fats: 28.5 g; Protein: 22.5 g

78
Grilled Chicken

15 minutes   15 minutes   4

Ingredients

- 4 chicken breasts, skinless and boneless
- 1 1/2 teaspoon of dried oregano
- 1 teaspoon of paprika
- 5 garlic cloves, minced
- 1/2 cup of fresh parsley, minced
- 1/2 cup of olive oil
- 1/2 cup of fresh lemon juice
- Pepper
- Salt

Directions

1. Add lemon juice, oregano, paprika, garlic, parsley, and olive oil to a large zip-lock bag. Season chicken with pepper and salt and add to bag. Seal bag and shake well to coat chicken with marinade. Let sit chicken in the marinade for 20 minutes.
2. Remove chicken from marinade and grill over medium-high heat for 5-6 minutes on each side. Serve and enjoy.

Nutrition: Calories: 293; Fats: 16.5 g; Protein: 33.1 g; Carbohydrates: 3.8 g

79
Curried Pork Tenderloin in Apple Cider

10 Minutes   26 minutes   6

Ingredients

- 16 ounces of pork tenderloin, cut into 6 pieces
- 1 1/2 tablespoons of curry powder
- 1 tablespoon of extra-virgin olive oil
- 2 medium onions, chopped
- 2 cups of apple cider, organic and unsweetened
- 1 tart apple, peeled and chopped into chunks

Directions

1. In a bowl, season the pork with the curry powder and set it aside.
2. Heat oil in a pot over medium flame.
3. Sauté the onions for one minute until fragrant.
4. Stir in the seasoned pork tenderloin and cook for 5 minutes or until lightly golden.
5. Add in the apple cider and apple chunks.
6. Close the lid and bring to a boil.
7. Allow simmering for 20 minutes.

Nutrition: Calories: 241; Protein: 23.2 g; Carbohydrates: 10.8 g; Fats: 10.3 g

80
Baked Salmon Foil Packets with Vegetables

15 minutes

15 minutes

4

Ingredients

- 1 pound of salmon (cut into 4 6-ounce fillets)
- 1/2 pound of asparagus (trimmed, then cut in half)
- 1/2 teaspoon of sea salt
- 1 tablespoon of fresh dill (chopped)
- 1/4 cup of olive oil
- 2 garlic cloves (minced)
- 10 ounces of grape tomatoes
- 1/4 teaspoon of black pepper
- 1 tablespoon of lemon juice and 1/2 tablespoon of zest
- 10 ounces of zucchini (sliced into half-moons)
- 1 tablespoon of fresh parsley (chopped)

Directions

1. Preheat the oven to 400°F or preheat the grill to medium. Layout 4 large squares of foil [at least 12x12 inches (30x30 cm)]. Put a salmon fillet in the center of each piece of foil. Divide the veggies squarely among the foil around the salmon.
2. Mix the olive oil, black pepper, parsley, sea salt, lemon juice, minced garlic, lemon zest, and dill in a small bowl. Put half of the oil mixture to skirmish the salmon, getting most of the garlic onto the salmon.
3. Pour the residual oil mixture on the veggies. Put more salt plus pepper on the salmon and veggies. Fold the foil and seal it to form packets. Place onto a baking sheet. Bake for 15-20 minutes, or grill (enclosed) for 13-18 minutes.

Nutrition: Calories: 392; Fats: 22.4 g; Protein: 31.6 g; Carbohydrates: 16.8 g

81
Garlic and Pumpkin Soup

15 minutes   **5 hours**   **4**

Ingredients

- 1 pound of pumpkin chunks
- 1 onion, diced
- 2 cups of vegetable stock
- 1 2/3 cups of coconut cream
- 1/2 stick almond butter
- 1 teaspoon of garlic, crushed
- 1 teaspoon of ginger, crushed
- Pepper to taste

Directions

1. Add all the fixing into your Slow Cooker. Cook for 4-6 hours on high. Puree the soup by using your immersion blender. Serve and enjoy!

Nutrition: Calories: 299; Fats: 22.1 g; Carbohydrates: 20.1 g; Protein: 5.2 g

82
Buttery Garlic Shrimp

10 minutes   **15 Minutes**   **4**

Ingredients

- 6 Tablespoons Butter
- 1 lb. Shrimp, Cooked
- 2 Lemons, Halved
- ½ Teaspoon Red Pepper Flakes
- 4 Cloves Garlic, Crushed
- Sea Salt & Black Pepper to Taste

Directions

1. Start by heating your oven to 425, and then place your butter in an eight-inch baking dish. The butter should melt.
2. Sprinkle your shrimp with salt and pepper, and then slice your lemon halves into thin slices.
3. Add your shrimp, garlic and butter into your baking dish. Sprinkle with red pepper flakes, cooking for fifteen minutes. Stir halfway through, and then squeeze the lemon wedges across the dish before serving.

Nutrition: Calories: 240; Protein: 18.8 g; Fats: 17.4g; Carbohydrates: 2.4 g

83
Golden Mushroom Soup

15 minutes   **8 hours**   **6**

Ingredients

- 1 onion, finely chopped
- 1 carrot, peeled and finely chopped
- 1 fennel bulb, finely chopped
- 1 pound of fresh mushrooms, quartered
- 8 cups of Vegetable Broth, Poultry Broth, or store-bought (low-sodium)
- 1/4 cup of dry sherry
- 1 teaspoon of dried thyme
- 1 teaspoon of garlic powder
- 1/2 teaspoon of sea salt
- 1/8 teaspoon of freshly ground black pepper

Directions

1. In your slow cooker, combine all the ingredients, mixing to combine.
2. Cover and set on low. Cook for 8 hours.

Nutrition: Calories: 148; Fats: 3.4 g; Carbohydrates: 21.3 g; Protein: 7.3 g

84
Grilled Flank Steak with Lime Vinaigrette

 **10 Minutes**   **10 minutes**   **6**

Ingredients

- 2 tablespoons of lime juice, freshly squeezed
- 2 tablespoons of extra virgin olive oil
- 1/2 teaspoon of ground black pepper
- 1/4 cup of chopped fresh cilantro
- 1 tablespoon of ground cumin
- 1/4 teaspoon of red pepper flakes
- 3/4 pound of flank steak

Directions

1. Heat the grill to Low-Medium heat
2. In a food processor, place all ingredients except for the cumin, red pepper flakes, and flank steak. Pulse until smooth. This will be the vinaigrette sauce. Set it aside.
3. Season the flank steak with ground cumin and red pepper flakes and allow to marinate for at least 10 minutes.
4. Place the steak on the grill rack and cook for 5 minutes on each side. Cut into the center to check the doneness of the meat. You can also insert a meat thermometer to check the internal temperature.
5. Remove from the grill and allow to stand for 5 minutes.
6. Slice the steak to 2 inches long and toss the vinaigrette to flavor the meat.
7. Serve with salad if desired.

Nutrition: Calories: 161; Protein: 14.3 g; Carbohydrates: 1.1 g; Fats: 11.5 g

85
Greek Baked Cod

| 9 minutes | 13 minutes | 4 |

Ingredients

- 1 1/2 pounds of Cod fillet pieces (4-6 pieces)
- 5 garlic cloves, peeled, and minced
- 1/4 cup of chopped fresh parsley leaves

Lemon Juice Mixture:

- 5 tablespoons of fresh lemon juice
- 5 tablespoons of extra virgin olive oil
- 2 tablespoons of melted vegan butter

For Coating:

- 1/3 cup of all-purpose flour
- 1 teaspoon of ground coriander
- 3/4 teaspoon of sweet Spanish paprika
- 3/4 teaspoon of ground cumin
- 3/4 teaspoon of salt
- 1/2 teaspoon of black pepper

Directions

1. Preheat the oven to 400°F
2. Scourge lemon juice, olive oil and melted butter. Set it aside
3. In another shallow bowl, mix all-purpose flour, spices, salt, and pepper, and set next to the lemon bowl to create a station
4. Pat the fish fillet dry, then dip the fish in the lemon juice mixture then dip it in the flour mixture, brush off extra flour
5. In a cast-iron skillet over medium-high heat, add 2 tablespoons of olive oil
6. Once heated, add in the fish and sear on each side for color, but do not thoroughly cook, remove from heat
7. With the remaining lemon juice mixture, add the minced garlic and mix
8. Drizzle all over the fish fillets
9. Bake for 10 minutes, until it begins to flake easily with a fork
10. Allow the dish to cool completely
11. Distribute among the containers, store for 2-3 days
12. To serve: Reheat in the microwave for 1-2 minutes or until heated through. Sprinkle chopped parsley. Enjoy!

Nutrition: Calories: 389; Carbohydrates: 10.9; Fats: 24.1 g; Protein: 31.3 g

86
Quick Shrimp Scampi

5 minutes   **10 minutes**   **4**

Ingredients

- 2 tablespoons of olive oil
- 1/2 cup of (120 ml) dry white wine
- 3 garlic cloves, minced
- 1 1/2 pound of (680 g) large shrimp, peeled and stroked dry
- Large pinch of crushed red pepper flakes
- 1 lemon, zested, one half cut into slices
- 1/8 salt
- 1/8 pepper
- 4 tablespoons of unsalted butter, slice into 4 pieces
- Large handful of fresh chopped flat-leaf parsley.

Directions

1. In a large skillet, warm up the oil over moderate heat. Flavor the shrimp with salt plus pepper, then put them in the skillet in a single coating. Cook, without interruption, until the shrimp's bottoms begin to turn pink, about 1 minute after.
2. Turnover the shrimp and cook until almost cooked through, about 1 minute more. Keep the shrimp on a plate and set it aside.
3. Adjust to medium, add the pepper flakes, garlic, and a little more oil if the pan seems dry; cook, repeatedly stirring until the garlic just begins to turn golden, about 1 minute. Add the wine, scraping up any burnt bits from the bottom of the pan, and simmer until most of the wine has vanished.
4. Mix in the butter, then season the sauce with lemon juice and salt from one lemon half. Add the cooked shrimp, the lemon zest, any juices accrued on the plate, and parsley and heave until the shrimp is warmed through, about 1 minute. Serve with lemon wedges, if you wish.

Nutrition: Calories: 355; Fats: 23.3 g; Carbohydrates: 6.4 g; Protein: 28.5

87
Ginger Soup

10 minutes

10 Minutes

4

Ingredients

- 1 Can Diced Tomatoes
- 1 Can Peppers
- 6 Cups Vegetable Broth
- 3 Cups Green Onions, Diced
- 2 Cups Mushrooms, Sliced
- 3 Teaspoons Garlic, minced
- 3 Teaspoons Ginger, Fresh & Grated
- 4 Tablespoons Tamari
- 2 Cups Bok Choy, Chopped
- 1 Tablespoon Cilantro, Chopped
- 3 Tablespoons Carrot Grated

Directions

1. Add all ingredients except for your carrot and green onion into a saucepan, and then bring it to a boil using medium-high heat.
2. Lower to medium-low, cooking for six minutes.
3. Stir in your carrots and green onions, cooking for another two minutes.
4. Serve with cilantro.

Nutrition: Calories: 89; Protein: 4.7 g; Fats: 1.2 g; Carbohydrates: 15.1 g

88
Fish Taco Bowls

10 minutes

15 Minutes

4

Ingredients

- 4 Tilapia Fillets, 5 Ounces Each
- 8 Teaspoons Tajin Seasoning Salt, Divided
- 2 Tablespoons Olive Oil
- 4 Cups Coleslaw Cabbage Mix
- 2 Tablespoons Red Pepper Miso Mayonnaise + Some for Serving
- 2 Avocados, Mashed
- Sea Salt & Black Pepper to Taste

Directions

1. Start by heating your oven to 425, lining a baking sheet with foil.
2. Rub your tilapia down with olive oil, and seasoning it.
3. Bake for fifteen minutes, and then allow it to cool.
4. In a bowl, combine your mayonnaise and coleslaw, and top with fish to serve. Add in your mashed avocado.

Nutrition: Calories: 382; Protein: 32.1 g; Fats: 25.5 g; Carbohydrates: 5.8 g

89
Creamy Broccoli Cauliflower Soup

10 minutes

6 hours

6

Ingredients

- 2 cups cauliflower florets, chopped
- 3 cups broccoli florets, chopped
- 3 1/2 cups chicken stock
- 1 large carrot, diced
- 1/2 cup shallots, diced
- 2 garlic cloves, minced
- 1 cup plain yogurt
- 6 oz cheddar cheese, shredded
- 1 cup coconut milk
- Pepper

Directions

1. Add all ingredients except milk, cheese, and yogurt to a crock pot and stir well.
2. Cover and cook on low for 6 hours.
3. Purée the soup using an immersion blender until smooth.
4. Add cheese, milk, and yogurt and blend until smooth and creamy.
5. Season with pepper and salt.
6. Serve and enjoy.

Nutrition: Calories 205,; Fats: 13.5 g; Carbohydrates: 12.4 g; Protein: 8.6 g

Chapter 4
APPETIZERS, SIDE DISHES AND SALADS

90
Thai Pasta Salad

| 15 minutes | 14 minutes | 8 |

Ingredients

- 1 (16-ounce) package dry spaghetti
- 2 tablespoons of peanut oil
- 1 medium yellow squash, julienned
- 1 medium zucchini, julienned
- 1 medium green bell pepper, julienned
- 1 red bell pepper, julienned
- 1 orange bell pepper, julienned
- 6 scallions, sliced
- 3 garlic cloves, minced
- 1 jalapeño pepper, minced
- 3/4 cup of chopped walnuts
- 1/3 cup of peanut oil
- 1 tablespoon of sesame oil
- 1/4 cup of unflavored rice vinegar
- 2 tablespoons of salt-free peanut butter
- 1 tablespoon of no-salt-added tomato paste
- 1/4 cup of chopped fresh cilantro
- 1 tablespoon of minced fresh ginger
- 1 teaspoon of sugar
- 1/4 teaspoon of salt-free chili seasoning

Directions

1. Cook the spaghetti in the pot with boiling water. Cook for 10 minutes, stirring once or twice. Remove from heat, drain, and set it aside.
2. Warm 2 tablespoons of peanut oil in a large sauté pan over medium heat. Add the julienned vegetables, scallions, garlic, jalapeño, and walnuts and cook, stirring, for 3-4 minutes.
3. Remove from heat and transfer to a huge bowl. Add cooked spaghetti. Whisk the remaining ingredients in a mixing bowl. Mix over the pasta salad. Serve immediately.

Nutrition: Calories: 390; Fats: 16.3 g; Protein: 9.1 g; Carbohydrates: 51.9 g

91
Whole-Wheat Couscous Salad with Citrus and Cilantro

15 minutes   2 minutes   6

Ingredients

- 1 1/2 cups of water
- 1 cup of whole-wheat couscous
- 1 medium cucumber, slice in halves
- 1-pint grape or cherry tomatoes halved
- 1 jalapeño pepper, minced
- 2 shallots, minced
- 2 scallions, sliced
- 2 garlic cloves, minced
- 2 tablespoons of freshly squeezed lemon juice
- 2 tablespoons of freshly squeezed lime juice
- 1 teaspoon of olive oil
- 1/4 cup of chopped fresh cilantro
- Freshly ground black pepper, to taste

Directions

1. Mix water into a saucepan and boil over high heat. Once boiling, stir in the couscous, reduce heat to medium-low, cover, and simmer for 2 minutes.
2. Remove pot from heat, remove the lid, and fluff couscous with a fork. Set it aside to cool for 5 minutes.
3. Scrape out the cucumber's seeds using a spoon, then dice and place them into a mixing bowl. Put the rest of the fixing in the bowl along with the cooked couscous and toss well to coat. Flavor with freshly ground black pepper, then serve immediately.

Nutrition: Calories: 113; Fats: 1.5 g; Protein: 3.7 g; Carbohydrates: 21.4 g

92
Simple Green Salad

5 minutes   5 minutes   4

Ingredients

- 1/4 cup of extra-virgin olive oil
- 1 tablespoon of fresh lemon juice
- 1/4 teaspoon of salt
- 1/4 teaspoon of freshly ground black pepper
- 6 cups of loosely packed mixed greens
- 1/2 small red onion, thinly sliced
- 1 small cucumber, peeled, and thinly sliced
- 1/4 cup of shredded Parmesan cheese

Directions

1. Mix the oil, lemon juice, salt, plus pepper in a small bowl. Store the dressing in 4 condiment cups. Mix the mixed greens, onion, and cucumber in a large bowl. Divide salad into 4 medium storage containers. Top each with 1 tablespoon of Parmesan cheese. To serve, toss the dressing and salad.

Nutrition: Calories: 172 g; Fats: 10.5 g; Carbohydrates: 16.7 g; Protein: 5.2 g

93
Tender Green Beans Salad

5 minutes   0 minutes   8

Ingredients

- 2 cups of green beans, trimmed, chopped, cooked
- 2 tablespoons of olive oil
- 2 pounds of shrimp, cooked, peeled
- 1 cup of tomato, chopped
- 1/4 cup of apple cider vinegar

Directions

1. Mix up all ingredients together.
2. Then transfer the salad to the salad bowl.

Nutrition: Calories: 152; Carbohydrates: 5.6 g; Fats: 5.5 g; Protein: 20.5 g

94
Kale-Poppy Seed Salad

10 minutes   5 minutes   6

Ingredients

- 1/2 cup of nonfat plain Greek yogurt
- 2 tablespoons of apple cider vinegar
- 1/2 tablespoon of extra-virgin olive oil
- 1 teaspoon of poppy seeds
- 1 teaspoon of sugar
- 4 cups of firmly packed finely chopped kale
- 2 cups of broccoli slaw
- 2 cups of thinly sliced Brussels sprouts
- 6 tablespoons of dried cranberries
- 6 tablespoons of hulled pumpkin seeds

Directions

1. Mix the yogurt, vinegar, oil, poppy seeds, and sugar in a small bowl. Store the dressing in 6 condiment cups.
2. In a large bowl, mix the kale, broccoli slaw, and Brussels sprout. Divide the greens into 6 large storage containers and top each salad with cranberries and pumpkin seeds. To serve, toss the greens with the poppy seed dressing to coat.

Nutrition: Calories: 103; Fats: 4.2 g; Carbohydrates: 10.3 g; Protein: 6.3 g

95
Southwestern Bean Salad with Creamy Avocado Dressing

15 minutes

0 minutes

4

Ingredients

- 1 head romaine lettuce, chopped
- 1 can of no-salt-added black beans, drained
- 2 cups of fresh corn kernels
- 2 cups of grape tomatoes, halved
- 2 small avocados, halved and pitted
- 1 cup of chopped fresh cilantro
- 1 cup of nonfat plain Greek yogurt
- 8 scallions, chopped
- 3 garlic cloves
- Quartered zest, and juice of 1 large lime
- 1/2 teaspoon of sugar

Directions

1. Mix the lettuce, beans, corn, and tomatoes in a large bowl. Toss you well combined. Divide the salad into 4 large storage containers. Put the avocado flesh into your blender or food processor.
2. Add the yogurt, scallions, garlic, lime zest and juice, and sugar. Blend until well combined. Divide the dressing into 4 condiment cups. To serve, toss the salad and the dressing.

Nutrition: Calories: 339 g; Fats: 8.8 g; Carbohydrates: 47.5 g; Protein: 17.4 g

96
Fajita Style Chili

10 minutes

5 hours

4

Ingredients

- 1 teaspoon of fajita seasoning
- 1 tablespoon of chili powder
- 1 pound of chicken breasts, boneless & cubed
- 1/2 teaspoon of cumin, ground
- 2 garlic cloves, minced
- Nonstick cooking spray as needed
- 2 cans (14.5 ounces of each) of tomatoes, diced
- 1/2 green bell pepper, julienned
- 1/2 red bell pepper, julienned
- 1/2 yellow bell pepper, julienned
- 1/2 onion, sliced
- 15 ounces of white kidney beans, rinsed & drained (canned)
- 3 tablespoons of sour cream
- 3 tablespoons of cheddar cheese, shredded & reduced fat
- 3 tablespoons of guacamole

Directions

1. Mix your chicken with fajita seasoning, garlic, cumin, and chili powder.
2. Grease a skillet and place it over medium heat. Add in your chicken, cooking until it's golden brown.
3. Transfer it to a slow cooker, and then add in your tomatoes with their juices, vegetables, and beans. Cover, and cook on low for five hours.
4. Garnish with guacamole, cheese, and sour cream before serving warm.

Nutrition: Calories: 462; Carbohydrates: 32.2 g; Fats: 17.5 g; Protein: 43.4 g

97
Persimmon Salad

10 minutes   **0 minutes**   **4**

Ingredients

- Seeds from 1 pomegranate
- 2 persimmons, cored and sliced
- 5 cups of baby arugula
- 6 tablespoons of green onions, chopped
- 4 navel oranges, cut into segments
- 1/4 cup of white vinegar
- 1/3 cup of olive oil
- 3 tablespoons of pine nuts
- 1 1/2 teaspoons of orange zest, grated
- 2 tablespoons of orange juice
- 1 tablespoon of coconut sugar
- 1/2 shallot, chopped
- Pinch cinnamon powder

Directions

1. In a salad bowl, combine the pomegranate seeds with persimmons, arugula, green onions, and oranges, and toss. In another bowl, combine the vinegar with the oil, pine nuts, orange zest, orange juice, sugar, shallot, and cinnamon, whisk well, add to the salad, toss and serve as a side dish.

Nutrition: Calories: 250; Carbohydrates: 34.3 g; Fats: 11.6 g; Protein: 2.7 g

98
Tart Apple Salad with Fennel and Honey Yogurt Dressing

 15 minutes 0 minutes 6

Ingredients

- 2 tart green apples, diced
- 1 small bulb fennel, chopped
- 1 1/2 cups of seedless red grapes, halved
- 2 tablespoons of freshly squeezed lemon juice
- 1/4 cup of low-fat vanilla yogurt
- 1 teaspoon of honey

Directions

1. Mix all the fixing into a mixing bowl, then serve immediately.

Nutrition: Calories: 70; Fats: 1.1 g; Protein: 2.1 g; Carbohydrates: 13.6 g

99
Radish and Olives Salad

5 minutes · 0 minutes · 4

Ingredients

- 2 green onions, sliced
- 1 pound of radishes, cubed
- 2 tablespoons of balsamic vinegar
- 2 tablespoons of olive oil
- 1 teaspoon of chili powder
- 1 cup of black olives, pitted and halved
- A pinch of black pepper

Directions

1. Mix radishes with the onions and the other ingredients in a large salad bowl, toss and serve as a side dish.

Nutrition: Calories: 137; Carbohydrates: 7.9 g; Fats: 9.8 g; Protein: 4.3 g

100
Smashed Brussels Sprouts

15 minutes   **40 minutes**   **6**

Ingredients

- 2 pounds of Brussels sprouts
- 3 garlic cloves, minced
- 3 tablespoons of balsamic vinegar
- 1/2 cup of extra virgin olive oil
- 1/2 teaspoon of black pepper, ground
- 1 leek washed and thinly sliced
- 1/2 cup of parmesan cheese, low sodium, grated

Directions

1. Warm the oven to 450°F and prepare two large baking sheets. Trim the yellow leaves and stems off of the Brussels sprouts and then steam them until tender, about twenty to twenty-five minutes.
2. Mix the garlic, black pepper, balsamic vinegar, and extra virgin olive oil in a large bowl. Add the steamed Brussels sprouts and leeks to the bowl and toss until evenly coated.
3. Spread the Brussels sprouts and leaks divided onto the prepared baking sheets.
4. Use a fork or a glass and press down on each of the Brussels sprouts to create flat patties. Put the Parmesan cheese on top and place the smashed sprouts in the oven for fifteen minutes until crispy. Enjoy hot and fresh from the oven.

Nutrition: Calories: 137; Carbohydrates: 8.7 g; Fats: 9.2 g; Protein: 5.8 g

101
Classic Hummus

5 minutes   **0 minutes**   **6-8**

Ingredients

- 1 (15-ounce) can of chickpeas, drained and rinsed
- 3 tablespoons of sesame tahini
- 2 tablespoons of olive oil
- 3 garlic cloves, chopped
- Juice of 1 lemon
- Salt
- Freshly ground black pepper

Directions

1. Mix all the ingredients until smooth but thick in a food processor or blender. Add water if necessary to produce smoother hummus. Store covered for up to 5 days.

Nutrition: Calories: 111 g; Fats: 5.7 g; Carbohydrate: 10.7 g; Protein: 4.1 g

102
Wedge Salad with Creamy Blue Cheese Dressing

15 minutes

0 minutes

4

Ingredients

- 1 cup of nonfat plain Greek yogurt
- Juice of 1/2 large lemon
- 1/4 teaspoon of freshly ground black pepper
- 1/4 teaspoon of salt
- 1/3 cup of crumbled blue cheese
- 2 heads romaine lettuce, stem end trimmed, halved lengthwise
- 1 cup of grape tomatoes, halved
- 1/2 cup of slivered almonds

Directions

1. Mix the yogurt, lemon juice, pepper, salt, and cheese in a small bowl. Store the dressing in 4 condiment cups. Divide the lettuce halves and tomatoes among 4 large storage containers. Store the almonds separately.
2. To serve, arrange a half-head of romaine on a plate and top with the tomatoes. Sprinkle with 2 tablespoons of almonds and drizzle with the dressing.

Nutrition: Calories: 183 g; Fats: 11.8 g; Carbohydrates: 8.2 g; Protein: 11.3 g

103
Avocado Side Salad

10 minutes   **0 minutes**   **4**

Ingredients

- 4 blood oranges, slice into segments
- 2 tablespoons of olive oil
- Pinch red pepper, crushed
- 2 avocados, peeled, cut into wedges
- 1 1/2 cups of baby arugula
- 1/4 cup of almonds, toasted and chopped
- 1 tablespoon of lemon juice

Directions

1. Mix the oranges with the oil, red pepper, avocados, arugula, almonds, and lemon juice in a bowl, then serve.

Nutrition: Calories: 260; Carbohydrates: 14.3 g; Fats: 20.8 g; Protein: 4.1 g

104
Delicious Lemon Chicken Salad

15 minutes   **5 minutes**   **4**

Ingredients

- 1 pound of chicken breast, cooked and diced
- 1 tablespoon of fresh dill, chopped
- 2 teaspoons of olive oil
- 1/4 cup of low-fat yogurt
- 1 teaspoon of lemon zest, grated
- 2 tablespoons of onion, minced
- 1/4 teaspoon of pepper
- 1/4 teaspoon of salt

Directions

1. Put all the fixing into the large mixing bowl and toss well. Season with pepper and salt. Cover and place in the refrigerator. Serve chilled and enjoy.

Nutrition: Calories: 215; Fats: 9.4 g; Protein: 29.2 g; Carbohydrates: 2.8 g

105
Corn Salad with Lime Vinaigrette

 15 minutes

 7 minutes

 6

Ingredients

- 4 1/2 cups of corn kernels, fresh
- 1 tablespoon of lemon juice
- 1 red bell pepper, diced
- 1 cup of grape tomatoes halved
- 1/4 cup of cilantro, chopped
- 1/4 cup of green onion, chopped
- 1 jalapeno, diced
- 1/4 red onion, thinly sliced
- 1/2 cup of feta cheese
- 2 tablespoons of Truvia baking blend
- 2 tablespoons of extra virgin olive oil
- 1/2 tablespoon of honey
- 3 tablespoons of lime juice
- 1/8 teaspoon of black pepper, ground
- 1/8 teaspoon of cayenne pepper, ground
- 1/8 teaspoon of garlic powder
- 1/8 teaspoon of onion powder

Directions

1. To create your lime vinaigrette, add the lime juice, onion powder, garlic powder, black pepper, cayenne pepper, and honey to a bowl. Mix, then slowly add in the extra virgin olive oil while whisking vigorously.
2. Boil a pot of water and add in the lemon juice, Baking Truvia, and corn kernels. Allow the corn to boil for seven minutes until tender. Strain the boiling water and add the corn kernels to a bowl of ice water to stop the cooking process and cool the kernels. Drain off the ice water and reserve the corn.
3. Add the tomatoes, red pepper, jalapeno, green onion, red onion, cilantro, and cooked corn to a large bowl and toss it until the vegetables are well distributed. Add the feta cheese and vinaigrette to the vegetables and then toss until well combined and evenly coated. Serve immediately.

Nutrition: Calories: 210; Carbohydrates: 25.8 g; Fats: 6.7 g; Protein: 11.3 g

106
Black-Eyed Peas and Greens Power Salad

15 minutes   6 minutes   2

Ingredients

- 1 tablespoon of olive oil
- 3 cups of purple cabbage, chopped
- 5 cups of baby spinach
- 1 cup of shredded carrots
- 1 can of black-eyed peas, drained
- Juice of 1/2 lemon
- 1/4 teaspoon Salt
- Freshly ground black pepper

Directions

1. In a medium pan, add the oil and cabbage and sauté for 1 to 2 minutes on medium heat. Add in your spinach, and cover for 3 to 4 minutes on medium heat, until greens are wilted. Remove from the heat and add to a large bowl.
2. Add in the carrots, black-eyed peas, and a splash of lemon juice. Season with salt and pepper, if desired. Toss and serve.

Nutrition: Calories: 312; Fats: 5.1 g; Carbohydrate: 48.4 g; Protein: 18.3 g

107
Chunky Black-Bean Dip

5 minutes   1 minute   2

Ingredients

- 1 (15-ounce) can of black beans, drained, with liquid reserved
- 1/2 can of chipotle peppers in adobo sauce
- 1/4 cup of plain Greek yogurt
- Freshly ground black pepper

Directions

1. Combine beans, peppers, and yogurt in a food processor or blender and process until smooth. Add some of the bean liquid, 1 tablespoon at a time, for a thinner consistency. Season to taste with black pepper. Serve.

Nutrition: Calories: 275; Fats: 3.4 g; Carbohydrate: 42.1 g; Protein: 18.5 g

108
Mixed Vegetarian Chili

10 minutes   36 minutes   4

Ingredients

- 1 tablespoon of olive oil
- 14 ounces of canned black beans, rinsed and drained
- 1/2 cup of yellow onion, chopped
- 12 ounces of extra-firm tofu, cut into pieces
- 14 ounces of canned kidney beans, rinsed and drained
- 2 cans of (14 oz) diced tomatoes
- 3 tablespoons of chili powder
- 1 tablespoon of oregano
- 1 tablespoon of chopped cilantro (fresh coriander)

Directions

1. Take a soup pot and heat olive oil in it over medium heat. Add onions and sauté for 6 minutes until soft. Add tomatoes, beans, chili powder, oregano, and beans. Boil it first, then reduce the heat to a simmer. Cook for 30 minutes, then add cilantro. Serve warm.

Nutrition: Calories: 340; Fats: 5.6 g; Carbohydrates: 47.6 g; Protein: 26.3 g

109
Colored Iceberg Salad

10 minutes | **0 minutes** | **4**

Ingredients

- 1 iceberg lettuce head, leaves torn
- 6 bacon slices, cooked and halved
- 2 green onions, sliced
- 3 carrots, shredded
- 6 radishes, sliced
- 1/4 cup of red vinegar
- 1/4 cup of olive oil
- 3 garlic cloves, minced
- Pinch black pepper

Directions

1. Mix the lettuce leaves with the bacon, green onions, carrots, radishes, vinegar, oil, garlic, and black pepper in a large salad bowl, toss, divide between plates and serve as a side dish.

Nutrition: Calories: 184; Carbohydrates: 11.3 g; Fats: 13.8 g; Protein: 3.8 g

110
Berry Salad with Shrimps

7 minutes | **0 minutes** | **4**

Ingredients

- 1 cup of corn kernels, cooked
- 1 endive, shredded
- 1 pound of shrimp, cooked
- 1 tablespoon of lime juice
- 2 cups of raspberries, halved
- 2 tablespoons of olive oil
- 1 tablespoon of parsley, chopped

Directions

1. Put all ingredients from the list above in the salad bowl and shake well.

Nutrition: Calories: 204; Carbohydrates: 12.2 g; Fats: 8.1 g; Protein: 21.5 g

111
Sliced Mushrooms Salad

10 minutes **20 minutes** **4**

Ingredients

- 1 cup of mushrooms, sliced
- 1 tablespoon of margarine
- 1 cup of lettuce, chopped
- 1 teaspoon of lemon juice
- 1 tablespoon of fresh dill, chopped
- 1 teaspoon of cumin seeds

Directions

1. Melt the margarine in the skillet.
2. Add mushrooms and lemon juice. Sauté the vegetables for 20 minutes over medium heat.
3. Then transfer the cooked mushrooms to the salad bowl, and add lettuce, dill, and cumin seeds.
4. Stir the salad well.

Nutrition: Calories: 58; Carbohydrates: 4.7 g; Fats: 3.1 g; Protein: 2.9 g

112
Black Pepper Baby Potatoes

10 minutes **3 hours** **12**

Ingredients

- 3 pounds of baby potatoes, halved
- 7 garlic cloves, minced
- 2 tablespoons of olive oil
- 1 tablespoon of rosemary, chopped
- A pinch of black pepper

Directions

1. In your slow cooker, mix oil with potatoes, garlic, rosemary, and pepper, toss, cover, cook on High for 3 hours, divide between plates and serve.

Nutrition: Calories: 137; Carbohydrates: 26.9 g; Fats: 2.1 g; Protein: 2.3 g

113
Cilantro Brussel Sprouts

10 minutes | 3 hours | 12

Ingredients

- 1 cup of red onion, chopped
- 1/4 cup of natural apple juice, unsweetened
- 2 pounds of Brussels sprouts, trimmed and halved
- 3 tablespoons of olive oil
- 1 tablespoon of cilantro, chopped
- A pinch of black pepper

Directions

1. In your slow cooker, mix Brussels sprouts with onion, oil, cilantro, pepper, and apple juice, toss, cover, and cook on Low for 3 hours.
2. Toss well, divide between plates and serve as a side dish.

Nutrition: Calories: 55; Carbohydrates: 6.4 g; Fats: 3.1 g; Protein: 1.7 g

114
Oregano Salad

10 minutes | 3 hours | 4

Ingredients

- 1 pound of tomatoes, cut into wedges
- 1 tablespoon of olive oil
- 1/2 teaspoon of garlic powder
- 1/2 teaspoon of sweet paprika
- 1/2 teaspoon of chili powder
- 1/2 teaspoon of onion powder
- 1 cup of low-sodium veggie stock
- 2 tablespoons of oregano, chopped

Directions

1. In the slow cooker, combine the tomatoes with the oil, garlic powder and the other ingredients. Put the lid on, and cook on Low for 3 hours.
2. Divide the mix between plates and serve as a side dish.

Nutrition: Calories: 75; Carbohydrates: 7.7 g; Fats: 4.1 g; Protein: 1.8 g

115
Radicchio Mix

10 minutes   6 hours   8

Ingredients

- 38 ounces of canned cannellini beans, no-salt-added, drained and rinsed
- 19 ounces of canned fava beans, no-salt-added, drained and rinsed
- 1 yellow onion, chopped
- 3 tomatoes, chopped
- 2 cups of spinach
- 1 cup of radicchio, torn
- 1/4 cup of basil, chopped
- 4 garlic cloves, minced
- 1 1/2 teaspoon of Italian seasoning
- 1 tablespoon of olive oil

Directions

1. In your slow cooker, mix cannellini beans with fava beans, oil, basil, onion, garlic, Italian seasoning, tomato, spinach, and radicchio, toss, cover, and cook on Low for 6 hours, divide between plates and serve as a side dish.

Nutrition: Calories: 271; Carbohydrates: 48.8 g; Fats: 1.3 g; Protein: 16.3 g

116
Green Side Salad

10 minutes   0 minutes   4

Ingredients

- 4 cups of baby spinach leaves
- 1 cucumber, sliced
- 3 ounces of broccoli florets
- 3 ounces of green beans, blanched and halved
- 3/4 cup of edamame, shelled
- 1 1/2 cups of green grapes, halved
- 1 cup of orange juice
- 1/4 cup of olive oil
- 1 tablespoon of cider vinegar
- 2 tablespoons of parsley, chopped
- 2 teaspoons of mustard
- A pinch of black pepper

Directions

2. In a salad bowl, combine the baby spinach with cucumber, broccoli, green beans, edamame, and grapes, and toss.
3. Add orange juice, olive oil, vinegar, parsley, mustard, and black pepper, toss well, divide between plates and serve as a side dish.
4. Enjoy!

Nutrition: Calories: 147; Fats: 6.4 g; Carbohydrates: 17.5 g; Protein: 4.2 g

117
Herbed Baked Zucchini

10 minutes **20 minutes** **4**

Ingredients

- 4 zucchinis, quartered lengthwise
- 1/2 teaspoon of thyme, dried
- 1/2 teaspoon of oregano, dried
- 1/2 cup of low-fat parmesan, grated
- 1/2 teaspoon of basil, dried
- 1/4 teaspoon of garlic powder
- 2 tablespoons of olive oil
- 2 tablespoons of parsley, chopped
- A pinch of black pepper

Directions

1. Arrange zucchini pieces on a lined baking sheet, add thyme, oregano, basil, garlic powder, oil, parsley, and black pepper, and toss well.
2. Sprinkle parmesan on top, introduce it to the oven and bake at 350°F for 20 minutes.
3. Divide between plates and serve as a side dish.
4. Enjoy!

Nutrition: Calories: 137; Fats: 7.4 g; Carbohydrates: 12.4 g; Protein: 5.1 g

118
Cilantro Salad

10 minutes **8 minutes** **4**

Ingredients

- 1 tablespoon of avocado oil
- 1 pound of shrimp, peeled, and deveined
- 2 cups of lettuce, chopped
- 1 tablespoon of balsamic vinegar
- 1 tablespoon of lemon juice
- 1 cup of fresh cilantro, chopped

Directions

1. Heat up a pan with the oil over medium heat, add the shrimps and cook them for 4 minutes per side or until they are light brown.
2. Transfer the shrimp to the salad bowl and add all remaining ingredients from the list above. Shake the salad.

Nutrition: Calories: 146; Carbohydrates: 3.7 g; Fats: 7.5 g; Protein: 17.8 g

119
Asparagus Salad

 10 minutes   15 minutes   3

Ingredients

- 10 ounces of asparagus
- 1 tablespoon of olive oil
- 1/2 teaspoon of white pepper
- 4 ounces of feta cheese, crumbled
- 1 cup of lettuce, chopped
- 1 tablespoon of canola oil
- 1 teaspoon of apple cider vinegar
- 1 tomato, diced

Directions

1. Preheat the oven to 365°F.
2. Place asparagus in the tray, sprinkle with olive oil and white pepper and transfer to the preheated oven. Cook it for 15 minutes.
3. Meanwhile, put crumbled Feta in the salad bowl.
4. Add chopped lettuce and diced tomato.
5. Sprinkle the ingredients with apple cider vinegar.
6. Chill the cooked asparagus to room temperature and add to the salad.
7. Shake the salad gently before serving.

Nutrition: Calories: 179; Fats: 11.6 g; Carbohydrates: 10.3 g; Protein: 8.8 g

120
Tuscan-Style Tuna Salad

 15 minutes   0 minutes   4

Ingredients

- 2 6-ounce cans of chunk light tuna, drained
- 1/4 teaspoon of salt
- 10 cherry tomatoes
- 2 tablespoons of lemon juice
- 4 scallions, trimmed and sliced
- 2 tablespoons of extra-virgin olive oil
- 1 15-ounce can of small white beans
- Freshly ground pepper

Directions

1. Mix tuna, beans, scallions, tomatoes, juice, oil, lemon, pepper, and salt in a medium bowl. Stir gently. Refrigerate until ready to serve.

Nutrition: Calories: 280; Fats: 10.8 g; Carbohydrates: 22.8 g; Protein: 24.3 g

121
Warm Kale Salad

15 minutes   **12 minutes**   **4**

Ingredients

- 2 teaspoons of olive oil
- 1 small red onion, diced
- 2 garlic cloves, minced
- 1 small red bell pepper, diced
- 8 cups of chopped kale
- Juice of 1 fresh orange
- 1 medium carrot, shredded
- 1/4 teaspoon of ground cumin
- 1/8 teaspoon of dried red pepper flakes
- 1 teaspoon of grated orange zest
- Freshly ground black pepper, to taste

Directions

1. Heat up oil in a large skillet or sauté pan over medium. Add the onion and cook, stirring, for 2 minutes. Add the garlic, bell pepper, kale, and orange juice and stir well to combine. Adjust heat to medium-low, cover, and cook for 5 minutes.
2. Remove lid, add remaining ingredients, and stir well to combine. Cover and cook for another 5 minutes. Remove from heat and serve immediately.

Nutrition: Calories: 148; Fats: 2.7 g; Protein: 5.2 g; Carbohydrates: 25.6 g

122
Tabbouleh Salad

15 minutes   **0 minutes**   **4**

Ingredients

- 2/3 cup of dry couscous
- 1 cup of boiling water
- 1 small ripe tomato, diced
- 1 small green bell pepper, diced
- 1 shallot, finely diced
- 1/3 cup of chopped fresh parsley
- 1 garlic clove, minced
- Juice of 1 fresh lemon
- 1 tablespoon of olive oil
- 1/2 teaspoon of freshly ground black pepper

Directions

1. Mix the dry couscous into a small bowl. Mix in the boiling water, cover, and set it aside for 5 minutes. Place the tomato, green pepper, shallot, and parsley into a salad bowl.
2. Mix the garlic, lemon juice, oil, and pepper in a small mixing bowl. Put the cooked couscous in the salad bowl. Put the dressing over the top and stir well to combine. Serve immediately.

Nutrition: Calories: 124; Fats: 3.1 g; Protein: 3.7 g; Carbohydrates: 20.4 g

123
Tuna Salad–Stuffed Tomatoes with Arugula

 5 minutes

 15 minutes

 4

Ingredients

- 1 teaspoon of dried thyme
- 3 tablespoons of sherry vinegar
- 3 tablespoons of extra-virgin olive oil
- 1/3 cup of chopped celery
- 1/4 teaspoon of freshly ground pepper
- 4 large tomatoes
- 8 cups of baby arugula
- 1/4 cup of finely chopped red onion
- 1/4 teaspoon of salt
- 1/4 cup of chopped Kalamata olives
- 2 5-ounce cans of chunk light tuna in olive oil, drained
- 1 can of great northern beans, rinsed

Directions

1. Whisk oil, salt, vinegar, and pepper in an average-sized bowl. Put 3 tablespoons of the dressing in a big bowl and set it aside.
2. Slice enough off the top of each tomato to remove the core, chop enough of the tops to equal 1/2 cup and add to the average-sized bowl. Scoop out the soft tomato tissue using a teaspoon of or melon baller and discard the pulp
3. Add tuna, onion, thyme, olives, and celery to the average-sized bowl; gently toss to mix. Fill the scooped tomatoes with the tuna mixture. Add beans and arugula to the gauze in the large bowl and toss to combine. Divide the salad into four plates and top each with a stuffed tomato.

Nutrition: Calories: 351; Fats: 14.6 g; Carbohydrates: 31.9 g; Protein: 24.0 g

124
Tuna Bowl with Kale

4 minutes   18 minutes   6

Ingredients

- 3 tablespoons of extra virgin olive oil
- 1 1/2 teaspoons of minced garlic
- 1/4 cup of capers
- 2 teaspoons of sugar
- 15-ounce can of drained and rinsed great northern beans
- 1 pound of chopped kale with the center ribs removed
- 1/2 teaspoon of ground black pepper
- 1 cup of chopped onion
- 2 1/2 ounces of drained sliced olives
- 1/4 teaspoon of sea salt
- 1/4 teaspoon of crushed red pepper
- 6 ounces of tuna in olive oil, do not drain

Directions

1. Place a large pot, like a stockpot, on your stove and turn the burner to high heat.
2. Fill the pot about 3-quarters of the way full of water and let it come to a boil.
3. Cook the kale for 2 minutes.
4. Drain the kale and set it aside.
5. Set the heat to medium and place the empty pot back on the burner.
6. Add the oil and onion. Sauté for 3 to 4 minutes.
7. Combine the garlic into the oil mixture and sauté for another minute.
8. Add the capers, olives, and red pepper.
9. Cook the ingredients for another minute while stirring.
10. Pour in the sugar and stir while you toss in the kale. Mix all the ingredients thoroughly and ensure the kale is thoroughly coated.
11. Cover the pot and set the timer for 8 minutes.
12. Put off the heat and stir in the tuna, pepper, beans, salt, and any other herbs that will make this one of the best Mediterranean dishes you've ever made.

Nutrition: Calories: 242; Fats: 11.7 g; Protein: 14.9 g; Carbohydrates: 19.5

125
Sour Cream Green Beans

10 minutes   4 hours   8

Ingredients

- 15 ounces of green beans
- 14 ounces of corn
- 4 ounces of mushrooms, sliced
- 11 ounces of cream of mushroom soup, low-fat and sodium-free
- 1/2 cup of low-fat sour cream
- 1/2 cup of almonds, chopped
- 1/2 cup of low-fat cheddar cheese, shredded

Directions

1. In your slow cooker, mix the green beans with the corn, mushrooms soup, mushrooms, almonds, cheese, and sour cream, toss, cover, and cook on Low for 4 hours. Stir one more time, divide between plates and serve as a side dish.

Nutrition: Calories: 251; Carbohydrates: 34.3 g; Fats: 8.7 g; Protein: 9.4 g

126
Cumin Brussels Sprouts

10 minutes   3 hours   4

Ingredients

- 1 cup of low-sodium veggie stock
- 1 pound of Brussels sprouts, trimmed and halved
- 1 teaspoon of rosemary, dried
- 1 teaspoon of cumin, ground
- 1 tablespoon of mint, chopped

Directions

1. In your slow cooker, combine the sprouts with the stock and the other ingredients, and cook on Low for 3 hours. Serve.

Nutrition: Calories: 76; Carbohydrates: 12.4 g; Fats: 1.6 g; Protein: 2.4 g

127
Peach and Carrots

10 minutes   6 hours   6

Ingredients

- 2 pounds of small carrots, peeled
- 1/2 cup of low-fat butter, melted
- 1/2 cup of canned peach, unsweetened
- 2 tablespoons of cornstarch
- 3 tablespoons of stevia
- 2 tablespoons of water
- 1/2 teaspoon of cinnamon powder
- 1 teaspoon of vanilla extract
- A pinch of nutmeg, ground

Directions

1. In your slow cooker, mix the carrots with the butter, peach, stevia, cinnamon, vanilla, nutmeg, and cornstarch mixed with water, toss, cover, and cook on Low for 6 hours. Toss the carrots one more time, divide between plates and serve as a side dish.

Nutrition: Calories: 130; Carbohydrates: 19.4 g; Fats: 5.2 g; Protein: 1.8 g

Chapter 5

SNACKS

128
Easy Seed Crackers

10 minutes

60 minutes

72 crackers

Ingredients

- 1 cup of boiling water
- 1/3 cup of chia seeds
- 1/3 cup of sesame seeds
- 1/3 cup of pumpkin seeds
- 1/3 cup of flaxseeds
- 1/3 cup of sunflower seeds
- 1 tablespoon of Psyllium powder
- 1 cup of almond flour
- 1 teaspoon of salt
- 1/4 cup of coconut oil, melted

Directions

1. Preheat your oven to 300°F.
2. Line a cookie sheet with parchment paper and keep it on the side.
3. Add listed ingredients (except coconut oil and water) to the food processor and pulse until ground.
4. Transfer to a large mixing bowl and pour melted coconut oil and boiling water, mix.
5. Transfer mix to prepared sheet and spread into a thin layer.
6. Cut dough into crackers and bake for 60 minutes.
7. Cool and serve.
8. Enjoy!

Nutrition: Calories: 88; Carbohydrates: 1.8 g; Protein: 3.1 g; Fats: 7.6 g

129
Spiced Up Pumpkin Seeds Bowls

10 minutes

20 minutes

4

Ingredients

- 1/2 tablespoon of chili powder
- 1/2 teaspoon of cayenne
- 2 cups of pumpkin seeds
- 2 teaspoons of lime juice

Directions

1. Spread pumpkin seeds over a lined baking sheet, and add lime juice, cayenne, and chili powder.
2. Toss well.
3. Preheat your oven to 275°F.
4. Roast in your oven for 20 minutes and transfer to small bowls.
5. Serve and enjoy!

Nutrition: Calories: 197; Fats: 18.3 g; Carbohydrates: 1.7 g; Protein: 6.2 g

130
Crispy Potato Skins

2 minutes | **19 minutes** | **2**

Ingredients

- 2 russet potatoes
- Cooking spray
- 1 teaspoon of dried rosemary
- 1/8 teaspoon of freshly ground black pepper

Directions

1. Preheat the oven to 375°F. Prick or pierce the potatoes all over using a fork. Put on a plate. Cook on full power in the microwave for 5 minutes. Flip over, and cook again for 3 to 4 minutes more, or until soft.
2. Carefully—the potatoes will be very hot—scoop out the pulp of the potatoes, leaving a 1/8 inch of potato pulp attached to the skin. Set it aside.
3. Spray the inside of each potato with cooking spray. Press in the rosemary and pepper. Place the skins on a baking sheet and bake in a preheated oven for 5 to 10 minutes until slightly browned and crispy. Serve immediately.

Nutrition: Calories: 120; Fats: 0 g; Carbohydrate: 27.3 g; Protein: 2.8 g

131
Roasted Chickpeas

5 minutes | **30 minutes** | **2**

Ingredients

- 1 (15-ounce can) chickpeas, drained and rinsed
- 1/2 teaspoon of olive oil
- 2 teaspoons of your favorite herbs or spice blend
- 1/4 teaspoon of salt

Directions

1. Preheat the oven to 400°F.
2. Wrap a rimmed baking sheet with paper towels, place the chickpeas on it in an even layer, and blot with more paper towels until most of the liquid is absorbed.
3. In a medium bowl, gently toss the chickpeas and olive oil until combined. Sprinkle the mixture with the herbs and salt and toss again.
4. Place the chickpeas back on the baking sheet and spread in an even layer. Bake for 30 to 40 minutes, until crunchy and golden brown. Stir halfway through. Serve.

Nutrition: Calories: 241 g; Fats: 3.8 g; Carbohydrate: 31.6 g; Protein: 19.4 g

132
Stuffed Avocado

10 minutes | 0 minute | 2

Ingredients

- 1 avocado, halved and pitted
- 10 ounces canned tuna, drained
- 2 tablespoons sun-dried tomatoes, chopped
- 1 and ½ tablespoon basil pesto
- 2 tablespoons black olives, pitted and chopped
- Salt and black pepper to the taste
- 2 teaspoons pine nuts, toasted and chopped
- 1 tablespoon basil, chopped

Directions

1. Using a bowl, mix the tuna with the sun-dried tomatoes. Add the rest of the ingredients except the avocado, then stir.
2. Stuff the avocado halves using the tuna mix and serve as an appetizer.

Nutrition: Calories: 305; Fats: 23.0 g; Carbohydrates: 5.4 g; Protein: 19.6 g

133
Hummus with Ground Lamb

10 minutes | 15 minute | 8

Ingredients

- 10 ounces hummus
- 12 ounces lamb meat, ground
- ½ cup pomegranate seeds
- ¼ cup parsley, chopped
- 1 tablespoon olive oil
- Pita chips for serving

Directions

1. Heat up a pan with the oil over medium-high heat, add the meat, and brown for 15 minutes stirring often.
2. Spread the hummus on a platter, spread the ground lamb all over, also spread the pomegranate seeds and the parsley and serve with pita chips as a snack.

Nutrition: Calories: 158; Fats: 8.7 g; Carbohydrates: 9.4 g; Protein: 11.5 g

134
Wrapped Plums

5 minutes

0 minutes

8

Ingredients

- 2 ounces prosciutto, cut into 16 pieces
- 4 plums, quartered
- 1 tablespoon chives, chopped
- A pinch of red pepper flakes, crushed

Directions

1. Wrap each plum quarter in a prosciutto slice. Put them all on a platter, then sprinkle the chives and pepper flakes all over. Serve and serve.

Nutrition: Calories: 35;; Fats: 1.2 g; Carbohydrates: 4.5 g; Protein: 2.3 g

135
Cucumber Sandwich Bites

5 minutes

0 minutes

12

Ingredients

- 1 cucumber, sliced
- 8 slices whole wheat bread
- 2 tablespoons cream cheese, soft
- 1 tablespoon chives, chopped
- ¼ cup avocado, peeled, pitted and mashed
- 1 teaspoon mustard
- Salt and black pepper to the taste

Directions

1. Spread the mashed avocado on each bread slice. Then spread the rest of the ingredients except for the cucumber slices.
2. Divide the cucumber slices on the bread slices and cut each slice in thirds. Arrange them on a platter and serve as an appetizer.

Nutrition: Calories: 78; Fats: 2.4 g; Carbohydrates: 11.5 g; Protein: 3.2 g

136
Cucumber Rolls

5 minutes | 0 minutes | 6

Ingredients

- 1 big cucumber, sliced lengthwise
- 1 tablespoon parsley, chopped
- 8 ounces canned tuna, drained and mashed
- Salt and black pepper to the taste
- 1 teaspoon lime juice

Directions

1. Put cucumber slices on a working surface and divide the rest of the ingredients. Roll them.
2. Place all the rolls on a platter and serve as an appetizer.

Nutrition: Calories: 79; Fats: 4.9 g; Carbohydrates: 2.6 g; Protein: 5.8 g

137
Olives and Cheese Stuffed Tomatoes

10 minutes | 0 minutes | 24

Ingredients

- 24 cherry tomatoes, top cut off and insides scooped out
- 2 tablespoons olive oil
- ¼ teaspoon red pepper flakes
- ½ cup feta cheese, crumbled
- 2 tablespoons black olive paste
- ¼ cup mint, torn

Directions

1. Using a bowl, combine the olives paste with the rest of the ingredients except for the cherry tomatoes, then mix well.
2. Stuff the cherry tomatoes using this mixture. Arrange them all on a platter and serve as an appetizer.

Nutrition: Calories:24; Fats: 1.6 g; Carbohydrates: 1.2 g; Protein: 1.1 g

138
Tomato Salsa

5 minutes	0 minutes	6

Ingredients

- 1 garlic clove, minced
- 4 tablespoons olive oil
- 5 tomatoes, cubed
- 1 tablespoon balsamic vinegar
- ¼ cup basil, chopped
- 1 tablespoon parsley, chopped
- 1 tablespoon chives, chopped
- Salt and black pepper to the taste
- Pita chips for serving

Directions

1. Using a bowl, combine the tomatoes with the garlic and the rest of the ingredients except for the pita chips. Then stir, divide into small cups and serve putting the pita chips on the side.

Nutrition: Calories: 77; Fats: 6.7 g; Carbohydrates: 3.1 g; Protein: 1.2g

139
Chili Mango and Watermelon Salsa

5 minutes	0 minutes	12

Ingredients

- 1 red tomato, chopped
- Salt and black pepper to the taste
- 1 cup watermelon, seedless, peeled and cubed
- 1 red onion, chopped
- 2 mangos, peeled and chopped
- 2 chili peppers, chopped
- ¼ cup cilantro, chopped
- 3 tablespoons lime juice
- Pita chips for serving

Directions

1. In a bowl, mix the tomato with the watermelon, the onion and the rest of the ingredients except the pita chips and toss well.
2. Divide the mix into small cups and serve with pita chips on the side.

Nutrition: Calories: 31; Fats 0.5g; Carbohydrates: 5.4 g; Protein: 1.3 g

140
Creamy Spinach and Shallots Dip

10 minutes   0 minutes   4

Ingredients

- 1 pound spinach, roughly chopped
- 2 shallots, chopped
- 2 tablespoons mint, chopped
- ¾ cup cream cheese, soft
- Salt and black pepper to the taste

Directions

1. In a blender, mix the spinach with the shallots and the rest of the ingredients, then pulse well.
2. Divide into small bowls and serve as a party dip.

Nutrition: Calories: 114; Fats: 5.5 g; Carbohydrates: 7.2 g; Protein: 8.9 g

141
Feta Artichoke Dip

10 minutes   30 minutes   8

Ingredients

- 8 ounces artichoke hearts, drained and quartered
- ¾ cup basil, chopped
- ¾ cup green olives, pitted and chopped
- 1 cup parmesan cheese, grated
- 5 ounces feta cheese, crumbled

Directions

1. Using your food processor, combine the artichokes with the basil and the rest of the ingredients, then pulse well. Transfer the mixture to a baking dish.
2. Introduce in the oven, bake at 375° F for 30 minutes, then serve as a party dip.

Nutrition: Calories: 75; Fats: 5.4 g; Carbohydrates: 3.6 g; Protein: 3.5 g

142
Avocado Dip

5 minutes   **0 minutes**   **8**

Ingredients

- ½ cup heavy cream
- 1 green chili pepper, chopped
- Salt and pepper to the taste
- 4 avocados, pitted, peeled and chopped
- 1 cup cilantro, chopped
- ¼ cup lime juice

Directions

1. Take a blender, mix the cream with the avocados and the rest of the ingredients and pulse well.
2. Divide the mixture obtained into bowls and serve cold as a party dip.

Nutrition: Calories: 145; Fats: 13.8 g; Carbohydrates: 4.1 g; Protein: 2.6 g

143
Goat Cheese and Chives Spread

10 minutes   **0 minute**   **4**

Ingredients

- 2 ounces goat cheese, crumbled
- ¾ cup sour cream
- 2 tablespoons chives, chopped
- 1 tablespoon lemon juice
- Salt and black pepper to the taste
- 2 tablespoons extra virgin olive oil

Directions

1. Using a bowl, combine the goat cheese with the cream and the rest of the ingredients, then mix really well.
2. Keep the mixture in the fridge for 10 minutes and serve as a party spread.

Nutrition: Calories: 181; Fats: 17.5 g; Carbohydrates: 2.9 g; Protein: 3.6 g

Chapter 6
DESSERT

144
Berry Blast

15 minutes   **40 minutes**   **2**

Ingredients

- 4 cups of blueberries (2 cups of fresh and 2 cups of frozen)
- 1 cup of rolled oats
- 1 teaspoon of cinnamon
- 1 tablespoon of all-purpose flour
- 2 teaspoons of unsalted butter
- 1 tablespoon of maple syrup

Directions

1. Coat a pie pan with cooking spray and set it aside. Put the blueberries on the pie plate. Preheat the oven to 250°Fahrenheit.
2. Combine the flour, butter, oats, maple syrup, and cinnamon in a large mixing bowl and whisk until you obtain a grainy mixture.
3. Transfer the oats mixture to the pie pan and bake for forty minutes until the mixture is golden brown. Serve warm.

Nutrition: Calories: 407 g; Fats: 9.1 g; Carbohydrates: 73.3 g; Protein: 7.9 g

145
Oats and Fruit Bar Cracker

15 minutes   **0 minutes**   **6**

Ingredients

- 1 cup of quinoa
- 1 cup of oats
- 1/2 cup of figs (dried)
- 1/2 cup of honey
- 1/2 cup of almonds (chopped)
- 1/2 cup of apricots (dried)
- 1/2 cup of wheat germ
- 1/2 cup of pineapple (dried and chopped)
- 1 tablespoon of cornstarch

Directions

1. Mix the fixing in a mixing bowl until you obtain a well-balanced mixture. Put the batter on a baking tray or plate and flatten it. Ensure that the mixture is at least one inch thick. Let it cool before you cut it into pieces and serve.

Nutrition: Calories: 335 g; Fats: 7.8 g; Carbohydrates: 57.1 g; Protein: 8.1 g

146
Colorful Pops

15 minutes | 0 minutes | 6

Ingredients

- 2 cups of watermelon, strawberries, and cantaloupe (diced)
- 2 cups of pure apple juice
- 2 cups of fresh blueberries
- 6 craft sticks
- 6 paper cups

Directions

1. Mix all the fruit in a mixing bowl. Divide the fruit salad into the paper cups and pour the apple juice. Ensure that the apple juice only covers half the paper cup. Deep-freeze the cups for an hour or until they are partially frozen.
2. Remove the cups and add the sticks to the cups, and deep freeze for one more hour. Serve them as colorful pops!

Nutrition: Calories: 79 g; Fats: 0.2 g; Carbohydrates: 18.3 g; Protein: 0.7 g

147
Low Calories Apple Pie

10 minutes | 10 minutes | 4

Ingredients

- 5 apples, cored, peeled, and roughly chopped
- 1/2 cup of water
- 1 tablespoon of maple syrup
- 1/2 a teaspoon of nutmeg, ground
- 2 teaspoons of cinnamon powder
- 1 cup of old-fashioned rolled oats
- 4 tablespoons of fat-free butter, melted
- 1/4 cup of coconut sugar

Directions

1. Add apples to your pressure cooker alongside water, cinnamon, maple syrup, and nutmeg.
2. Toss well.
3. Take a bowl and add butter, oats, sugar, and whisk.
4. Spread over apple mix.
5. Lock the lid and cook on HIGH pressure for 10 minutes.
6. Release the pressure naturally for 10 minutes.
7. Open the lid and transfer to serving plates.
8. Serve and enjoy!

Nutrition: Calories: 238; Fats: 5.6 g; Carbohydrates: 43.8 g; Protein: 4.5 g

148
Grilled Plums with Vanilla Bean Frozen Yogurt

10 minutes

15 minutes

4

Ingredients

- 4 large plums, sliced in half and pitted
- 1 tablespoon of olive oil
- 1 tablespoon of honey
- 1 teaspoon of ground cinnamon
- 2 cups of vanilla bean frozen yogurt

Directions

1. Preheat the grill to medium heat. Brush the plum halves with olive oil. Grill, flesh-side down, for 4 to 5 minutes, then flip and cook for another 4 to 5 minutes, until just tender.
2. Mix the honey plus cinnamon in a small bowl. Scoop the frozen yogurt into 4 bowls. Place 2 plum halves in each bowl and drizzle each with the cinnamon-honey mixture.

Nutrition: Calories: 215; Fats: 9.8 g; Carbohydrates: 28.9 g; Protein: 2.3 g

149
Mixed Fruit Compote Cups

5 minutes

15 minutes

2

Ingredients

- 1 1/4 cup of water
- 1/2 cup of orange juice
- 12 ounces of mixed dried fruit
- 1 teaspoon of ground cinnamon
- 1/4 teaspoon of ground ginger
- 1/4 teaspoon of ground nutmeg
- 4 cups of vanilla frozen yogurt, fat-free

Directions

9. Mix your dried fruit, nutmeg, cinnamon, water, orange juice, and ginger in a saucepan. Cover, and allow it to cook over medium heat for ten minutes. Remove the cover and then cook for another ten minutes. Add your frozen yogurt to serving cups, and top with the fruit mixture.

Nutrition: Calories: 259; Fats: 6.0 g; Carbohydrates: 46.4 g; Protein: 4.1 g

150
Ginger and Pumpkin Pie

10 minutes

2 hours

10

Ingredients

- 2 cups of almond flour
- 1 egg, whisked
- 1 cup of pumpkin puree
- 1 1/2 teaspoons of baking powder
- Cooking spray
- 1 tablespoon of coconut oil, melted
- 1 tablespoon of vanilla extract
- 1/2 teaspoon of baking soda
- 1 1/2 teaspoons of cinnamon powder
- 1/4 teaspoon of ginger, ground
- 1/3 cup of maple syrup
- 1 teaspoon of lemon juice

Directions

1. In a bowl, flour with baking powder, baking soda, cinnamon, ginger, egg, oil, vanilla, pumpkin puree, maple syrup, and lemon juice, stir and pour in your slow cooker greased with cooking spray and lined with parchment paper, cover the pot and cook on Low for 2 hours and 20 minutes.
2. Leave the pie to cool down, slice, and serve.

Nutrition: Calories: 123; Carbohydrates: 7.8 g; Fats: 8.8 g; Protein: 3.6 g

Chapter 7

21 DAYS MEAL PLAN

DAY	Breakfast	Lunch	Dinner
1	Avocado & Spinach Smoothie	Chicken Tortillas	Brown Rice Pilaf
2	Pineapple Smoothie	Butternut-Squash Macaroni and Cheese	Chicken Corn Chowder
3	Salmon and Egg Scramble	Lemon and Cilantro Rice	Jerk Beef and Plantain Kabobs
4	Breakfast Fruits Bowls	Roasted Carrot Soup	Beef Stew with Fennel and Shallots
5	Pear & Greens Smoothie	Healthy Chicken Orzo	Zucchini Tomato Bake
6	Creamy Oats, Greens & Blueberry Smoothie	Grilled Mahi-Mahi with Artichoke Caponata	Curried Pork Tenderloin in Apple Cider
7	Sweet Berries Pancake	Artichoke and Spinach Chicken	Baked Salmon Foil Packets with Vegetables
8	Chia Seeds Breakfast Mix	Stuffed Portobello	Grilled Flank Steak with Lime Vinaigrette
9	Refreshing Mango and Pear Smoothie	Grilled Fennel-Cumin Lamb Chops	Crab, Zucchini, and Watermelon Soup
10	Spinach Muffins	Tofu Turkey	Lemon Herb Baked Salmon
11	Banana Bread	Baby Spinach and Grains Mix	Grilled Chicken
12	Blackberry and Apple Smoothie	Rosemary Roasted Chicken	Portobello-Mushroom Cheeseburgers
13	Cinnamon and Pumpkin Porridge Medley	Poached Salmon with Creamy Piccata Sauce	Chilled Cucumber and Avocado Soup with Dill
14	Buckwheat Crepes	Healthy Vegetable Fried Rice	Greek Baked Cod

15	Avocado Cup with Egg	Vegetable Cheese Cal- zone	Chicken & Rice Soup
16	Raspberry Smoothie	Red Beans and Rice	Fish Taco Bowls
17	Grapes & Kale Smooth- ie	Hearty Lentil Soup	Beef with Cucumber Raito
18	Pumpkin Muffins	Chicken with Potatoes Olives & Sprouts	Golden Mushroom Soup
19	Mixed Berries Smoothie	Black-Bean Soup	Quick Shrimp Scampi
20	Kiwi & Cucumber Smoothie	Loaded Baked Sweet Potatoes	Beef Pot
21	Quinoa Bowls	Spinach Casserole	Asian Pork Tenderloin

DISCOVER THE AMAZING BONUS
I HAVE IN STORE FOR YOU

Scan the QR Code or go to www.vitaminsmineralsguides.com
for instant access to a FREE life-saving guide that come with this Book:

FREE: A PRACTICAL 70+ PAGE GUIDEBOOK

Discover the vitamins and minerals that should never be missing from your diet - and which foods you can get them from-.

A free ultra-detailed report – suitable for beginners too – to discover all the essential nutrients for living a long and healthy life

Here is everything you will find in this guide

» What are vitamins and why are they essential
» Minerals - what they do and why you should never be missing them in your diet-
» The 8 signs that you are deficient in vitamins or minerals and how to remedy that
» 3 facts that (maybe) you won't know about vitamins and minerals
» And much much more...

Made in United States
Troutdale, OR
06/07/2023

10457182R10072